# DISCOVER:

Your Opportunities

How to Get Your Priorities Straight

The Miracles in Your Life

How You Can Turn Activity into Energy

Health and Happiness

Freedom

How to Bloom Where You Are Planted

Self-Love

Your Self-Confidence

The Power for Overcoming Defeat

Courage to Face Your Future

How Life Can Be Beautiful

---

Unlock the key to each of them in

*Discover Your Possibilities*

---

# DISCOVER YOUR POSSIBILITIES

*Robert H. Schuller*

**HARVEST HOUSE PUBLISHERS**
Irvine, California 92714

**DISCOVER YOUR POSSIBILITIES**

Copyright © 1978 by Robert H. Schuller

Published by Harvest House Publishers, Irvine, California 92714

Library of Congress Catalog Card Number 79-90780
ISBN 0-89081-214-4

**Printed in the United States of America.**

# Table of Contents

# Introduction

You can discover the tremendous possibilities still waiting to be uncovered in your life! But you must first become a possibility thinker. Every person is either a possibility thinker or an impossibility thinker. Possibility thinkers look at problems and see opportunities; look at barriers and see hurdles; look at frustrations and see amazing potential for growth. The difference is in your attitude!

I'm excited about the ideas God has allowed me to share with you. You will find exciting, powerful principles that will inspire you to discover how to be all you are meant to be. You can break the shackles of your limitations. Begin today to live on top of the mountain, seeing the sunlight and feeling the warmth of God's love. Your possibilities are unlimited!

Robert H. Schuller
Garden Grove, California

# *Discover Your Self-Confidence*

# 1

## *You Can Experience Self-Confidence*

In the beautiful movie, "The Sound of Music," Maria makes the decision to leave the convent and go work in the home of the Van Trapp family, with its seven children. She makes the break and is on her way to what she is certain is God's will for her life. On the way, she sings a beautiful song that speaks of her confidence.

If you will follow the advice in this book, then nothing will defeat you unless you lose your self-confidence!

A 16-year-old boy in Ghana, Africa, read the story of how the Garden Grove Community Church started with Mrs. Schuller as the first member. "Then I can start a church out here, too!" he reasoned. Six months after that positive idea burst into his inspired imagination, he had a congregation of sixty members. He has great plans! I'm taking him serious! You must always take positive thinking, positive acting, positive performing people seriously, for they will inevitably move mountains, make history and work miracles!

Paul Mosely is a 72-year-old member of my church. The week I wrote this chapter Mr. Mosely was held up by a robber in the bowling alley he manages. The thief bound his hands behind his back and fled with $10,000 in cash. Possibility thinker Mosely managed to summon help. How? By using his tongue to dial the telephone. Believe you can solve problems and you will. Bright ideas, creative thoughts, brilliant inspirations are generated when a person deeply believes that he can accomplish the impossible.

A 29-year old husband and father is suffering from multiple sclerosis. He listens to our weekly television program, "Hour of Power." The week after week dose of possibility thinking worked a miracle in his mental outlook. One day he burst out with self-confidence and declared to his wife, "I can! I know I can! I can become a doctor of veterinary medicine! Dr. Schuller says with faith in God I can, so I know I can!" Today, as I write this chapter, that young man is well on his way in his studies. He is going to succeed. Why am I so sure? Because he believes in himself!

A 16-year-old boy in Africa, a 72-year-old man in America, a 29-year-old student—all have one thing in common: All three have an enormous inner Spiritual Force and Power which thrusts and propels them onward and upward. This inner Spiritual Force is called *Self-confidence*.

## What Is Self-Confidence?

It is the God-power within you! There is a tremendous verse in the Bible which J.B. Phillips translates: "For it is God working in you giving you the will and the power to achieve His purpose." The good news I have for you is this: The Eternal Creative Force of the universe we call God can surge within your being to give you self-belief, self-esteem, self-love, self-confidence! Without it—you're sunk, with it—you're invincible!

Eliminate the unholy triad of negative emotions—inferiority, inadequacy, insignificance—wipe these destructive devils out of your mind with the positive power of self-confidence!

Someone gave me a cartoon showing a bum sitting on a park bench. His clothes are tattered, his toes are coming out of his shoes. He's the picture of the classic hobo. Underneath the sketch is this caption: "No man is completely worthless—he can always serve as a horrible example."

> ## YOUR SELF-IMAGE
> ## WILL SHAPE YOUR LIFE

Self-image psychology has proved that the picture you persistently hold of yourself will gradually mold and shape you into that person! Picture yourself as a cheerful person—you'll become a cheerful person! Picture yourself a fluent public speaker and you will become an eloquent public speaker!

Once Abraham Lincoln, refusing to hire a man, explained: "I don't like the looks of that man." An aide corrected him, "But Mr. President, the man can't help how he looks." To which the wiser Lincoln answered, "But he can! Thoughts and actions shape a man's eyes and a man's face!"

# 2

## *Here's How To Get Self-Confidence*

Here are five resources you can use to bolster your self-confidence.

### I.

*Psychiatrists* may help you. If your self-image is so negative that you find yourself entertaining suicidal thoughts, you should seek professional help. Depth analysis may help uncover some ego-damaging experiences in early childhood. By all means seek out a therapist who believes in belief!

## II.

*"Props"* can be self-confidence boosters. Where some people will need serious professional help in their pursuit of self-confidence, others may need only the help of simple "props." In his book, *The Devil's Advocate*, Morris West tells of one character who simply put a fresh carnation in the lapel of his coat and faced the world with confidence! A hair style will do the same for others. A new set of sharp clothes may do the trick for you. Perhaps you need to trim off a few pounds before you can begin to feel self-confident. Plastic surgery, Maxwell Maltz reported, transformed many a patient from a self-degrading to a self-complimenting person!

But remember! These are materialistic props. They may give your self-confidence a needed boost; however, a lasting self-confidence must have deeper spiritual roots to survive the fall and winter seasons of the soul's journey through life.

## III.

*People* who preach possibility thinking can do wonders in giving birth and bolstering power to self-confidence.

A world famous opera star was slated to perform in the Paris Opera House. The place was packed with fans eager to hear the famous performer. Just before the performance was to begin, the manager stepped in front of the curtain and announced: "We regret to inform you that the star you hoped to hear tonight is suffering from laryngitis and will not perform." An audible gasp of disappointment rose from the audience. "However," the announcer continued, "I'm pleased to introduce to you a new performer of great promise who will stand in for your evening's entertainment." The unknown singer performed his first selection with excellence. As he finished he was received with icy stillness by the disappointed audience. Nobody applauded! The darkened auditorium was cold, and insultingly quiet. Suddenly from an upper balcony came an enthusiastic child's voice, "Daddy, I think you were wonderful." Then it happened. Applause suddenly broke out, loud and long!

Little people can build big people's ego, and the reverse is true. President Theodore Roosevelt was proud of his first three sons when they announced their intention to join the military service. But when his fourth son also decided to go into uniform the tough, rough riding President resisted. "Not all my boys," he argued. To which his wife replied, "Ted, if you raise them as eagles you can't expect them to fly like sparrows."

The author and playwright, William Saroyan, was inspired to self-confidence at the age of 13. He had purchased a typewriter when his esteemed granduncle Garabed came down and visited him.

"My boy, what's that contraption?" the old gentleman asked.

"A typewriter, sir," the lad answered.

"What's it for?" Garabed inquired.

"For clear writing, sir." And William handed him a sample.

"What's this writing?" the granduncle asked.

"Philosophical sayings," William answered.

"Whose?" Uncle Garabed quizzed.

"Mine, sir," the youth affirmed.

The wise old fellow studied the sheet and then handed it back to his nephew and said, "Proceed, for it is not impossible to walk on water."

"I knew then I could do it," William Saroyan recalls. Self-confidence—strong enough to last him a lifetime— was born within him then and there!

## IV.

*Pluck,* that resourceful spirit that motivates an individual to risk failure in trying to do something on his own. This is what really builds self-confidence. Self-confidence cannot be bought, or taught, it must be caught! You catch it when you take a chance, and make it!

Try something small like learning to walk; the child takes first one faltering step, then the next, so you can build belief in yourself by starting small and as you succeed, take larger steps.

I am told that the suspension bridge over Niagara was built in this fashion. First a kite was flown across the foaming falls, attached to the kite was a thread, attached to the thread was a rope, attached to the rope was a cable. And so the cables, and the other pieces, were moved together until a great bridge spanned the chasm!

The story is told of two mountain men who sat on a log looking dreamily across the valley to a distant mountain range. One mountaineer was a huge man; the other was a small man. The following conversation took place between the little man (L.M.) and the big man (B.M.):

(L.M.)—"I'll bet there's big bears in them hills."

(B.M.)—"Uh huh."

(L.M.)—"I wish I was a big man like you. You know what I'd do if I was a big man like you?"

(B.M.)—"Huh-uh."

(L.M.)—"I'd go into them thar hills and catch me a big bear—and I'd tear him limb from limb! That's what I'd do if I was a big man like you!"

(B.M.)—Turning to face the little man: "There's plenty of little bears in them hills, too!"

Start small—and succeed. Succeed where you are—then move on to bigger things. "Lift where you stand," Edward Barrett wisely said.

---

## PLUCK IS TRYING HARDER THAN YOU EVER HAVE BEFORE

---

One mile from my offices in California is Disneyland—a fabulous success story. Few people ever demonstrated more self-reliance than Walt Disney. How did he get it? "When I was nearly 21 years old I went broke for the first time," Disney recalled. "I slept on cushions from an old sofa and ate cold beans out of a can. Then I set out for Hollywood, California." Reflecting on his subsequent success the Grand Man of Movieland uttered this priceless statement, "I didn't know what I couldn't do so I was willing to take a chance and try anything."

Remember the story of the boy who wanted so much to march in the circus parade? When the show came to town the bandmaster needed a trombonist, so the boy signed up. He hadn't marched a block when his horrible sounds created pandemonium. "Why didn't you tell me you couldn't play a trombone?" the bandmaster demanded. The boy answered simply, "How did I know? I never tried before!"

## V.

*Finding and following God's Plan* for your life is the soundest, surest way to self-confidence. It is also the best way to keep the feeling of self-confidence growing within you now!

# 3

# *Keeping Your Self-Confidence*

Anyone can keep their self-confidence if they will follow this simple formula:

Find and follow
God's Plan for your life!

Check, read, and reaffirm these power-generating Bible verses:

"Be confident in this one thing—That God who has begun a good work in you *shall complete it.*" (See Philippians 1:6).

Already God is revealing to you His plan for your life. He is stimulating your imagination as you read this book. He has started to work in your life. Be sure . . . God finishes what He starts!

"For it is God at work in you giving you the will and the power to achieve His purpose." (See Philippians 2:13).

As I write this chapter I have been reading the book by my friend, Lawrence Welk, *Wunnerful, Wunnerful.* The inspiring success story of this man's life reminds me of the Bible verse, "The eagle stirreth up her nest that the young might learn to fly." (Deuteronomy 32:11).

God often allows problems to shake us up in order to get us out of a rut and onto the beautiful road He has planned for us.

Lawrence might have grown up to spend his life as a farmer in North Dakota—except for a seemingly terrible thing that happened. He was a small boy on the edge of his teenage years when he woke up one morning deathly ill. He was taken to the nearest hospital 75 miles away. Here he was diagnosed as suffering from a ruptured appendix. Peritonitis had already set in. Poison ravaged his body. A tube was inserted in his side to siphon off the deadly pollution. Feverish days turned into frightening weeks. Delirious, he narrowly, miraculously survived.

Through the long months of recuperation in his country farmhouse he began to play sounds on his father's old accordion. Suddenly he began to believe in a Divine Plan for his life! "It seemed to me that God has given me a second chance at life and I prayed for guidance to use my life in ways that would please Him most." From that deep spiritual experience was born the God-inspired dream. "Now a thought so exciting, so overpowering that I could scarcely bear to think of it began to inch its way forward into my mind. Maybe I wouldn't have to be a farmer! I knew nothing of the life of a real musician, of course, but somehow I seemed to see myself standing in front of great crowds of people playing my accordion. They were smiling and happy—it was an intoxicating vision—and the more I played, the more real that vision became."

I have a young member of my church named Janet Randall. She wrote me the following letter recently.

"Dear Dr. Schuller: You are an inspiring person whom I admire very much. I enjoy your books and enjoy your sermons very much. You might remember me from meeting my mother once when she was in the hospital. Her name is Jane Randall.

"I am her oldest daughter, Janet. I, as you may remember, am half-blind, as my brother is mostly. My sister has perfect sight.

"I am 12, my brother 11 and my sister 9. I am in 7th grade, my brother in 6th and my sister in 4th.

"When we moved to California from Mississippi we had a troubled time. We are Baptist in religion but have changed to Prodestant (sic). Your church is what our family feels is what a church should be like.

"I have made a few little posters for you. I guess you know that schools do not permit religion to be brought in, so we had to write a composition on a great person to us. Guess what? I wrote about you. I have included the report that I had written."

Then she included her report which begins with these wise sentences. "Great people are just ordinary people with an extraordinary amount of determination . . . Greatness is a thing only given to those who deserve it by their kindness to others and faith in themselves." She went on to write her report on my work. She had the basic facts of my life correct: "When this person moved to California he had only a drive-in theatre for a church, $500 in money, and his wife for a member." She hit the nail on the head in her closing sentence: "Robert Schuller came from a poor family, living on a farm in Iowa. His parents taught him when he was young to have faith in God and to have confidence in himself."

I was, in fact, just five years old when I came to believe that God wanted me to be a Christian minister. It became an all consuming passion! Nothing and no one can stop the person who feels "called-by-God" to do what he's doing!

"For it is God at work in you giving you the will and the power to achieve His purpose." (See Philippians 2:13).

# 4

## *What You See Is What You'll Be*

From a day-to-day, week-to-week, life-living standpoint, nothing is more necessary than self-reliance, self-confidence, self-affirmation, self-esteem, self-affection and self-belief. If you have it, you are mentally and emotionally mature. But without it, God help those who have to live with you. Because without these attributes, a person either becomes a withering worm, or a rank, obnoxious egotist.

This story illustrates my point. A Major in the military was promoted to the rank of Colonel. But he was basically an insecure person who had never developed authentic self-confidence. He still needed props in order to maintain his self-esteem.

When he received his promotion, he was led into his

new office. Left alone, he sat down behind the large desk. No sooner had he dropped into his new chair in his plush quarters when the door opened and a young airman came in and saluted him.

In a desperate effort to try and impress this young recruit, the newly promoted Colonel said, "Just a minute, young man," as he picked up his telephone. "I have to answer my phone. It rang just before you stepped in." He picked up the telephone and in a pompous way said, "Oh, yes, General. Yes sir, General. Yes sir, I'll telephone the President immediately."

Then he put the phone down and looked at the young man and said, "What can I do for you?" The nervous youth answered, "Oh, nothing, sir. I just came in to connect your telephone, sir."

It is amazing how many people today are trying to make a big impression because deep down within themselves they lack the inner security that comes through self-affirmation and a positive self-image. Insecure people get themselves in all kinds of hot water.

We have already considered how you can get self-confidence and how you can keep that feeling of self-confidence. Now we will consider how you can put that feeling of self-confidence to work in your life.

But first, three things: a question, a Bible verse and a statement.

The question: *How do you see yourself today*? It would be a very healthy, though probably a torturingly painful test, if I asked you to sit down with a blank sheet of paper and a pencil and write a description of the kind of person you really are. Take some time now and do it. How do you see yourself today? What are your strengths? What are your weaknesses? What are your personality assets? What are your personality liabilities? What is your future going to be like?

Now the Bible verse:
"For as a man thinks in his heart, so is he." (See Proverbs 23:7).

And now the statement:
WHAT YOU SEE IS WHAT YOU'LL BE!
The picture you have of yourself in your mind is the kind of person you most certainly will become. So develop today the first steps toward a consistent self-confident, self-affirming, self-reliant, positive self-image! *Get it, keep it and use it!*

My thoughts are centered around three key words: The *need,* the *seed,* and the *creed* of self-confidence.

1. The *need* of self-confidence. How can you ever become the person God wants you to be if you can't believe in yourself?

The two words "I Can" are the most powerful, life-changing words you can repeat. In my home we have five children. Two of the most profane words we do not permit in our home are the words, "I Can't." Verbalize those negative words, and you surrender yourself to their negative, hypnotic power. They'll destroy you. By contrast, affirm, *"I Can!"* It's astounding what miracles you can accomplish.

A member of my church tells me he can remember as a young black boy living in more than thirteen foster homes in the south as he was growing up. He can remember falling asleep in school simply because he was undernourished. Now by every standard of judgment you would say that with those strikes against him he was destined for a crooked life of failure. But the man who adopted him said, "Just because you're black and poor doesn't mean you can't be beautiful." Birt Duncan earned his Ph.D. in psychology from Princeton University and is today completing his work for his M.D. degree from the University of California in San Diego.

"I Can," Birt Duncan said, and he did!

Shortly after I published one of my books, a lady telephoned me and asked, "Are you the Dr. Schuller who wrote *Move Ahead with Possibility Thinking?*" "I am," I replied. "Well," she said, "I'd like to meet you." I was hesitant to make a commitment over the telephone, but then she said, "I just want to see you to find out if you're a phoney or not." That did it. I decided I would see her.

The next morning my secretary buzzed me and said, "Barbara Bassinger is here, and she said you would see her." And into my office came the weirdest contraption I have ever seen in my life. There, in a wheelchair, was a huge body wrapped in steel, leather and chains, bolted, riveted and welded together. Flashing out of it all were two bright black eyes of what obviously was the pretty face of a twenty-four-year-old-girl. She could see I was shocked; I couldn't hide it. "I just wanted you to know that what you say is true," she said. *"If you believe, it's possible!* Say 'I Can'; and it works! I am a quadraplegic cerebral palsy. I was told I would never walk; it would be impossible. And I would never be able to have a normal education. I would be a mentally retarded, handicapped person all my life.

"I began to catch the power of faith as a child in Sunday School; that with God I could do anything. I went to a doctor and asked him to make braces for me, but he said, 'Not for quadraplegic cerebral palsies.' 'But Doctor,' I pleaded. 'It seems so simple. If you put a piece of iron between my ankles, my legs can't fly out.' So he did. Then I said, 'Doctor, I think if you put a chest plate here and some straps and iron bars to hold my head up and to stretch my neck, my head wouldn't fly around.' So he did. Then I said, 'Doctor, I think if you put a hinged bar between my wrists my arms wouldn't fly around.' And so he did. I simply invented what I'm wearing today. Dr. Schuller, it may look pretty bad, but let me show you something. *I can walk!"*

Lifting herself out of her wheelchair, she creaked and clanked around my office on the twelfth floor of the Tower of Hope, proud as a peacock and justly so, as she finally fell back into her wheelchair.

"I Can," Birt Duncan said, and he did it! "I Can," Barbara Bassinger said, and she did it!

"I Can," said Bert Blyleven. Bert is a member of my church, and I'm proud of him. I remember him when he was just a boy. Kids always laughed when he said he was going to be a major league baseball player. But, he said, "I Can." Bert visualized it, dreamed it and imagined it, and today he is one of the great ball players in the major leagues.

I saw him at the end of the baseball season, and I asked him, "How did you do?" "Well," he replied, "I've set some new records for the Minnesota Twins; a new record in strike outs in a season and a new record in the number of shut-outs pitched by any pitcher in a season." Isn't that great!

The *need* for self-confidence. Without it you can't go anyplace, do anything or be what God wants you to be.

So if you have a negative self-image of yourself, don't harbor it or hold on to it. Throw it away! Begin to see yourself as what you want to be. If you want to be a kind and gentle person, picture yourself smiling and being kind and gentle. If you want to be aggressive and enthusiastic, picture yourself being enthusiastic. If you want to be a good student, picture yourself as a very scholarly student, pouring through your books, working hard, and *you'll be that person!* If you want to be slim and trim, picture yourself slim and trim, and keep holding that picture in front of you. *What you see is what you'll be!* "*As a man thinketh in his heart, so is he.*"

2. The *seed* of self-confidence. How do you get it? There are several ways, but let me just submit a few that you can use and grab hold of. One way to develop self-confidence is to have a sense of belonging. I don't suppose anything gives a person an identity consciousness more than belonging. In fact, some psychologists insist, and I'm inclined to agree, that you can't really see yourself except in relation and relationships to others.

I have said that I believe *I can do anything I want to do, but I don't think I can do anything alone.* Jesus said, "*I am the vine, you are the branches; he who abides in Me, and I in him, he bears much fruit; for apart from Me you can do nothing."* (John 15:5) But I can do all things if I'm engrafted in Christ's power. I believe that!

Many people just don't have a strong positive self-image because they have an identity crisis. An identity comes through your sense of belonging.

A story is told of four boys who were playing ball in a sand lot in New York City. They took a break in their game and talked, of all things, about religion. One boy said, "I'm Catholic." Another boy said, "I'm a Protestant." And another boy said, "I'm a Jew." The fourth boy dropped his head in embarrassment and finally said, "I . . . I'm nothing" and went home.

If you're a father or mother and you don't belong to a church and you have children, join a church! Give your children the consciousness of belonging. You don't want them to feel like nothing!

There is a second thing that develops a sense of belonging, and that's an awareness of being God's child. Nothing can make you an emotionally, mentally healthy person quicker than an awareness that you really belong to God. This means *you* are important! *You are somebody* even if nobody knows your name!

Television and radio personality, Art Linkletter, told me about a time when he was interviewing a young boy on his program. He asked the little boy, "Do you have a dog?" And the boy answered, "Yes." "Does your dog do any tricks?" The boy said, "Yes." Then Mr. Linkletter asked, "Is it a pedigree?" And the boy replied, "I don't know. I'm Jewish!"

A sense of belonging. It's terribly important in the development of self-affirmation.

Fred Dienert recalled to me an incident in the life of our friend Billy Graham. He recalled the time twenty years ago in Portland, Oregon, when Billy was inspired to pray to God for wisdom and guidance on whether he should start a radio program. And so, in conversation with Fred Dienert, they came to the conclusion that they would need $25,000 to start that ministry. Billy immediately drew up a list of the biggest Christian names who could easily support it. He contacted these people, and to his astonishment they all let him down.

Now this is an interesting story, because I can relate to it. From time to time my church has gone through financial crises; starting with nothing in a drive-in theater, having to come up with a down payment on our land, etc. And many times I would secretly make a list of people who I knew could easily help, but invariably when I approached them I was disappointed. So I can identify with Billy Graham's plight.

Billy was so discouraged and depressed that he said to Fred, "I guess that's it. God doesn't want us to do it, because the big people are not coming up with the money." And then Fred Dienert, God bless him, said to Billy, *"Did you ever think of giving God's little people a chance?"* And so the closing night of the Portland crusade, it was announced that they were seeking God's will as to whether they should broadcast their program nationally, and if anyone felt they wanted to support it, they could send a dollar or two, or whatever they wanted, and Billy would know what to do. And you know what happened; the rest is history: $25,000 came in! It didn't come in hundreds or five hundreds or thousands. It came in $1's, $5's and $10's!

> GOD DOES HIS BIGGEST THINGS
> THROUGH HIS LITTLE PEOPLE!

That's a fact of history. Show me your biggest movements, your most successful programs for God and Jesus Christ, and they're not supported by huge foundations or multi-millionaires. They're made possible by God who does His biggest things through His little people.

The seed of self-confidence comes through a sense of belonging and through an awareness of being God's child. And it comes through a consciousness of the expectations that people have from you. When people expect you to be something and you know they expect it, that brings the best out of you.

The Harvard psychologist, Robert Rosenthal, tested this idea in an experiment. He told a school teacher in a controlled situation at the beginning of the school year, "We are conducting a psychological experiment. I want you to know that your students this year are all highly selected and exceptionally bright. You are very fortunate. We want to see how these students do this year." At the end of the semester all the students scored high —with almost an A average—exactly as the teacher expected them to do, because they were all selected because of their unusual intelligence.

At the end of the testing period the teacher was told the truth, and the truth was that her students were just average students picked at random. When the teacher thought they were outstanding students and expected so much from them, they rose to that expectation. It probably was the way the teacher talked to them and treated them, or the body language she used as she communicated to them; the whole composition of the mental climate. It's amazing.

There is a law that sums up my point this way: "I am not what I think I am. I am not what you think I am. I am what I think you think I am." We tend to rise to the expectations that people have of us.

The artist was painting an old beggar on the side of the street, and when the painting was done the old beggar looked at the picture and said, "Who's that?" (It was the picture of a handsome, intelligent, wonderful man.) The artist replied, "That's the *you* I see." The beggar looked again and said, "That's me? Then that's the man I'll be! He stood upright, threw his shoulders back and walked off."

> THE PERSON YOU SEE
> IS
> THE PERSON YOU'LL BE.

And so Goethe said, "Treat people as if they were what they ought to be and you help them to become what they are capable of being."

3. The *creed* of self-confidence. What is it? The creed of self-confidence is this: I affirm that I am made in the image of God, that Christ died for me and that I am God's redeemed child born again through the Holy Spirit, and that means I am somebody great! Therefore, I will never criticize and condemn God's handiwork and run myself down. And when I inevitably, as a human being, have self-degradating, self-flagellating or self-negative thoughts about myself, I will not verbalize these negative emotions, but I will counter attack them by affirming that I am a wonderful, unique person. God made me. Christ saved me. And the Holy Spirit fills me with His gifts. I'm a beautiful person!

I affirm that *every* person is a beautiful soul. I will never condemn a person to his face or say anything bad about him. I will never say, "You're stupid," "You're ugly," "You're ignorant," or "You're fat." I will never say anything that could give him a negative self-image of himself. That's the creed of self-confidence.

In one of my books, I tell the story of our Former Secretary of the Treasury, Romana Banuelos. We're proud of her here in California. She came to this state when she was twenty-two years of age. After her husband divorced her and abandoned her with her two little boys, she made her way on a bus to Los Angeles with $7 in her pocket and took a job making tacos early in the morning. Finally she saved and borrowed enough to buy the taco shop and began to make and sell more tacos.

Today her business is one of the largest Mexican wholesale businesses of Mexican products in the United

States. This year they say, she is doing nearly $10 million worth of business. The interview with her was very interesting. When asked what the major problem is that keeps Mexican-Americans down today, she answered: "They believe the lie they have been told about themselves—that Mexicans are inferior. I was raised as a child in Mexico, and no one can make me believe that lie! I'm proud of my Mexican ancestry! I taught my sons about the great Mexican heritage, and they don't act defeated. Here in America they make some of them feel like they're inferior.

"My little girl came home from school one day and asked, 'Are we Spanish or Mexican, Mommy?' I answered, 'Honey, we're Mexican.' She was very dismayed, because she picked up the idea in school that Spaniards were bright and beautiful and Mexicans were stupid.

"When I found that out I decided to take her to Mexico on a vacation at the next opportunity. When I did I showed her the magnificent pyramids, the wide streets, and the beautiful architecture. I said to her, 'This was done by your ancestors, the Aztecs.' Then I took her to some of the crowded towns, with narrow twisting little streets and said, 'This was designed by the Spanish conquerors. But the Aztecs are your ancestors! You are Mexican. You *are* somebody!' And when she came back to America she didn't want to be Spanish. She wanted to be Mexican!"

What you see is what you'll be! Absolutely! Don't ever do anything to tear a person down. Do you know that Jesus Christ saved the worst condemnation for people who tore others down? He called them vipers and snakes, because they were going around making people feel inferior!

On our church board we have a man named Dr. Floyd Baker, and I'm proud of him. He is a professor of physics in one of the universities here. His story is also in one of my books. When he was writing his thesis for his advanced degree, he made this confession:

"I first entered the teaching profession in 1960 and brought with me a set of attitudes toward instruction and student-teacher interaction. Now in retrospect, I had what I know today to be a bad attitude toward my students and their motivation. I recall I used to say to them at the beginning of the semester, 'You have to pass this course or you might as well change your major. I am the *only* one teaching this class, so you might as well get along as best you can. I don't like people who won't study, so get on the ball! I give you the material and all you have to do is learn it. Let me tell you, about 50 percent of you won't pass. Don't let it be you!'

"As you can see, I always gave the students superb confidence. Well, amazingly, my predictions always came true—50 percent flunked out—always, year after year. I would get together with the other college professors and we would drink coffee and we would laugh at the number of dropouts that we had in our classes. We used to say that the one who received the most dropouts was the most successful teacher. I know now that this is a bad attitude.

"About this time, my wife and I started attending a very dynamic church, the Garden Grove Community Church." And then he tells how he became a positive-thinking Christian in a deep way and how this began to change his attitude, until finally, with this new faith-attitude, he started the semester differently. He said to his students, "I want everyone of you to pass. And it's my job to see that you do. The material is difficult, but if we work together, every student in this class can pass and learn a great deal." Without changing his grading procedure one bit, at the end of that semester *every student passed!* There was only one C, one B minus, and all the rest got B's and A's in physics, of all things!

The *need* of self-confidence; you need it.
The *seed* of self-confidence; become God's child.

The *creed* of self-confidence; go out and build the confidence of others around you, and you'll do the work of Jesus Christ. And in the process, your own self-confidence will become stronger and stronger. YOU CAN!

# Discover Self-Love

# 1

## *The Language Of Love*

There are two kinds of people in the world. There are people who build walls and there are people who build bridges. Robert Frost said, "Before you build walls, make sure you know what you are walling out and what you are walling in." That's good advice for wall-builders, for in their defensiveness and hostility, they usually drive people away.

The bridge-builders are the people who expect the best in other people. They expect good to come out of others and are eager to believe the best, even in the worst situations. They build bridges because they have learned the language of love!

Which are you—a bridge builder or a wall-builder? Are you carrying resentments? How many fears, how many anxieties, how many worries are you suffering from because you will not forgive somebody who hurt you deeply? How many sunny days are turned gray by your angry mind, seething, quarrelling in fantasy bouts with your adversary—an ex-husband, an ex-wife, a relative, a customer, a client or a clerk?

Are you suffering from ulcers, arthritis, high blood pressure, or heart problems simply because you will not forgive? How many people are developing wrinkles in their skin that will become permanent creases, monuments to the fact that they spent most of their lives thinking angry thoughts, until the frown wrinkles work their way irreducibly into their countenance? And how many friends did you once have that no longer talk to you because you developed a reputation for pouting, grumbling and complaining because the daily resentments that got under your skin stayed there and infected your whole system?

The solution is to learn the language of love, and that language begins with these words from I Corinthians 13, the great love chapter:

"Love is not resentful" (verse 5)

Every winter in the Northeast part of our country, big, soft, fluffy, white snowflakes begin to flutter down. Winter is coming. Born and raised in Northwest Iowa, I can recall the first snow of the year. It was wonderful. But what we didn't appreciate were the blizzards, because the blizzards would come with driving winds of 50 to 60 miles an hour sometimes until they closed the roads with impassable drifts. We wouldn't be able to get

out to the store to buy our food. It was serious. One positive thing was I wouldn't have to go to school! I remember looking out of our farm house a half mile down the road to the hill where we could see the snow-plow cutting through the drifts—slicing it, chopping it up and blowing it into a huge, spewing stream into the ditch. After the snowplow came through, the road was open again, and we could go for our food. And I could go back to school.

Resentments are like snowdrifts, and forgiveness is the snowplow. You see, forgiveness in the eyes of the non-Christian is simply a matter of passive acquittal. But in the Christian context that's not it at all. In the Christian context forgiveness is the snowplow. It means opening the road and removing the barriers so that you can now communicate and listen again to what people are trying to say. We dialogue and interchange; we move back and forth. Whether it's between my God and myself or a person and myself, forgiveness is a snow-plow, not just an eraser on a chalkboard.

There are a lot of resentments that can build up in your life in a period of a day. And the only way to put joy back on your face is to find an overpowering love that can remove the resentments and fill you with for-giveness. "I forgive you," is the language of love.

Now, in order to conquer resentments; in order to submit to the forgiving spirit, let's understand what some of the obstacles are:

*Obstacle #1: An extreme sense of justice.*

I have had a problem with this myself. I have a strong sense of justice. I have to remind myself to re-member what the word of God says: *"Vengeance is mine,"* saith the Lord. (Deut. 32:35).

I have often been helped by the story of Joseph. He was sold by his brothers as a slave to Egypt. They had hoped they could send him away and get him out of their lives. He became, however, a ruler. They meant to kill him; instead they ended up in the providence of God crowning him. As Joseph said, "You meant it for evil, but God meant it for good." Let justice be handled by the Lord. He knows how to take care of people.

There was a man who was the victim of injustice who said to his pastor, "But wouldn't it be man-like of me to be angry?" And his pastor said, "Indeed it would. But it would be Christlike of you to forgive."

*Obstacle #2: Making a mountain out of a molehill.*

We tend, you know, to emphasize the little negative things that get under out skin and forget all the positive qualities. The person who has hurt you, no matter who he is, does have many fine qualities, but chances are, you can't see them.

Once, to illustrate this point, in a class I was teaching on Possibility Thinking, I took a sheet of paper and tacked it on a board. With a felt pen I made a small X right in the center of the sheet. And then I made a tiny circle and a short straight line on it. I asked members of my class to come up and tell me what they saw. One person said a line; another said a circle; others said an X. Every person came up; and when the class finished I said, "Not one of you said, 'I see a sheet of paper.' " The bulk of what I had tacked up was one big sheet of white paper. All they saw were the tiny black spots. They didn't see the mass of white.

We tend, by nature, to be negative thinkers. We see the wrong, and we don't see the good. We take a little detail and get hung up on it. That becomes an obstacle.

It's like an artist who was teaching his students how to paint. He took them out to paint a sunset. They set up their easels, and began to paint. Just as the sun was reaching its height of colorful glory, the instructor noticed that one student was lost in painting the shingles on a barn in the foreground of the pastoral scene. The teacher said, "Look, if you spend so much time painting the shingles, you will miss the sunset." Don't get so hung up on details of life to the point that you miss the big, beautiful picture.

# 2

## *The Possibilities Of Love*

The solution to wall-building and resentments is to
see the possibilities in any offensive experience. In other
words, wall-builders forget about all of the positive possibilities that are present in any offensive situation.
They overlook the fact that these situations are the
times you can best turn your scars into stars!

A few months ago I was on the East coast in a very
prominent city to deliver a sermon in a huge church on
Sunday morning. I had just arrived back in this country
the afternoon before from Europe. At the Geneva airport I had cashed my two $50.00 traveler's checks and
received two $50.00 bills in exchange. Mrs. Schuller
and I found a hotel where I could finish preparing my
sermon for the next morning. As I finished, she men-
tioned that a particular movie was playing in a theatre
nearby. I had reason to believe this movie might give

me some good sermon illustrations, so we went to the theatre. We stood in line—a long line—and just as we got to the ticket window, we could see that the movie was beginning in just a few minutes. I didn't want to miss the beginning.

As my turn came at the window, I gave them one of my $50.00 bills. The ticket teller looked at it and said, "I'm sorry, we don't take $50.00 bills." I said, "You can't reject it. Don't you know what that bill says? It says right here, 'This is legal tender for all debts public and private.' You cannot refuse it." (I was bold, for I had my tickets in my hand already.) But the gal said again, "I'm sorry, we can't take it."

Now never in my life have I been a public protester, but the line was getting restless behind me and it was beginning to drizzle—and the movie was beginning. I

said, "I'm sure you'll take it, because it's a good $50 bill." She said, "I'm sorry, we won't take it." The line got longer, and I was getting impatient. Finally she said, "You've got your tickets." "Alright," I said, "thank you," and I walked in. Then she stuck her neck out and yelled at the head usher, "That man didn't pay!" It happened to be in an area where I have a vast listening audience, and I thought, "Oh no, I hope nobody recognizes me." The usher stopped me and asked, "What's the big idea?" I told him, "She wouldn't take my $50 bill, and it's all I've got. I just left Geneva twelve hours ago, and I'm sorry. But you watch where I sit, and you just check with the hotel and see if there isn't a Robert Schuller listed there, and check out if they think he's honest or not. When I get out of the theatre, you'll have had time to check me out."

Unfortunately, halfway through the movie I had to step out to the men's room. I no sooner got in the men's room than there was that same usher standing right by me. "Okay," he said, "you are either the greatest counterfeit or the greatest con man I've ever met." "Did you check the hotel?" I questioned. "No," he said sternly. "I don't have to. I can spot a con man a mile off." "Look," I said, "here is the $50 bill. You take it, check it out, and when I leave the theatre, give me $45 back please. I want to go in and watch the movie." And I left him with the $50 bill.

When the movie was over, my wife and I walked out and I couldn't find the usher, but I saw a man in a black coat who looked like he was an official. I asked him, "I'm looking for the head usher. He's got my $50 bill." He looked at me and said, "Oh, you're the guy with the $50 bill! We don't take $50 bills here." "Well, I want my change, $45, or I want the $50 bill back," I persisted. Then he reached in his pocket, and with a terrible look on his face he said, "Here is your blankety-blank $50 bill," and he threw it on the floor. So I reached down and picked it up and put it in my pocket. And do you know what? I was mad! Which is not really a Christian emotion! Well, I prayed about it, but I was still offended at his behavior.

We walked out of the theatre into the rain. We had to walk three blocks to the hotel. My wife said to me, "Bob, this is a great opportunity to practice what you preach. This is loaded with possibilities." "It is?" I said, almost dreading her answer. "Like what?" "Well, let's go back to the hotel, break the bill at the hotel, come back here and pay them the $5. The usher will listen, and we will leave a witness for Jesus Christ." We got to the hotel, got change for the $50 bill and walked back to the theatre through the rain.

We knocked at the door since it was all closed up and kept knocking until the girl who ran the peanut stand opened the door. "Not you again," she said. "Please, can I see the head usher?" I asked. I went in just in time to see the usher coming down the steps carrying his tuxedo and wearing his street clothes. "Oh no, not you again," he protested. I said, "Yes, it is me again. I have come to pay you the $5 I owe you." "Oh, you didn't have to do that," he said. "I did have to do it," I answered. "I owe it to you. But now you owe me something. I want you to know that I'm doing this for one reason: I claim to be a Christian, and it's very exciting trying to follow Christ in daily life. I want you, for the rest of your life, to never forget that if you ever hear people say that Christians are all a bunch of hypocrites, that there's nothing to this Jesus Christ and there's nothing to this God business, I want you never to forget that once there was a man whom you didn't know who came in dripping wet out of the rain to pay his $5 because he said he was a Christian, and that makes a difference." His eyes were moist. He took the $5 and said, "Yes, sir. Thank you, sir. Good night, sir. I'm very sorry." And we smiled and shook hands.

Do you know what it means to forgive? To forgive doesn't just mean that you erase the slate. Forgiveness means you cut the road open and you move back and forth and you help each other. You don't just acquit the person. You see their possibilities and you make them into something beautiful. That can happen to you. But it can only happen when Jesus Christ comes into your life.

I don't think you can live in today's world and go through a day, to say nothing of a week or a month, without having the love of Christ in your heart to give you the kind of forgiving power you must have to succeed today and tomorrow.

# 3

## *The Power Of Love*

If forgiveness is the language of love, then fearlessness is the power of love. Wouldn't it be wonderful if something could happen deep within your mind to give you such inner confidence, security and calmness that you would never be afraid of anybody or anything ever again? Wouldn't it be fantastic if you had a mental and spiritual experience that would permanently give you an imperishable and invisible shield against anxiety, worry, fear and guilt? The truth is, if you have an experience with Perfect Love, you will conquer fear in your life forever.

"There is no fear in love, but perfect love casts out fear." (1 John 4:18)

What is very important is that we understand that there is such a thing as *imperfect* love, and there is such a thing as *perfect* love. All doctrines, all lectures, all sermons, all messages, all books, all songs—all of these things talk about an *imperfect* love. And that's part of our problem in the world today. Much of what we think of as love is only an imperfect form of the real thing—perfect love. Consider these three levels of love:

1. *"I love you because I need you."* This is imperfect love for it is basically selfish.
2. *"I love you because I want you."* This form of love is really nothing more than lust.
3. *"I love you because you need me."* This love is much closer to Christian love. The lover says, "I need to give myself away to people who need help. You need me, therefore I love you."

As you look at these three statements, you will see the difference between counterfeit love and authentic love; between imperfect love and perfect love. The essence of perfect love is to find a need and seek to fulfill that need—"I need to give myself away to people who need help. You need me, therefore I love you." The question is, where do you find that kind of love today?

Recently I passed through one of our great mid-American airports. I had just delivered a lecture to a college where they required all the students on the campus to read my book, *Self-Love, the Dynamic Force of Success.* I was asked to deliver a lecture on that subject and then to answer questions from the student body. It was a very enjoyable experience—one of those quick 24-hour, in and out-of-town trips. As I was changing planes in this beautiful airport, I stopped at a Fannie Mae Candy store.

I must hasten to say that I don't like candy. I used to like it, but I have psyched myself into believing I don't like it because that is the only way to lose weight. I don't diet. Do you know what a diet is? A diet is when you deprive yourself of something you want in order to reach an objective, at which point you reward yourself by giving yourself what you've denied yourself all the time you were dieting. And then you have to diet again.

So I decided the only way for me to lose weight, and

keep it off, was to lose my appetite for foods that would make me fat. Candy tends to make me fat, so I have programmed myself (I think!) not to like candy. I tell myself that the chocolate is probably either too bitter or it's too ghastly sweet. And if that doesn't work, I imagine that their creamy contents were probably put together under unsanitary conditions.

At any rate, I go through this whole mental rigama-role to convince myself that I can't stand candy. But I stopped in to buy some chocolates for my wife; she loves chocolates. She happens to particularly love chocolate-covered nuts. So I walked into this Fannie Mae store where a clerk in a white dress greeted me from behind the counter. There was another customer at the counter, an older woman, in a red dress with a flight bag and a little suitcase. She seemed to be indeci-sively window shopping. The woman in white wasn't doing anything to help her, so I said, "Do you have one-pound boxes of chocolate-covered nuts?"

And at that point the customer said, "Oh, sure. They've got one-pound boxes of all kinds of chocolate-covered nuts." I looked back at the clerk, who was, after all, the real authority. She could see that I was waiting for her to answer, so she said, "Yes, we can make up a one-pound box of any kind of chocolate-covered nuts."

"Maybe you can make up a one-pound box of tur-tles," I said, "those chocolate covered nuts with cara-mel." Again, the customer interrupted, "Yes, they have those in one-pound boxes. They also have those in three-pound boxes!" I looked at the clerk, waiting for a reply from the real authority, since I was not content with the doubtful opinion of just another plain cus-tomer. The clerk looked nervously at the customer who kept interrupting and finally said, "Yes, we do have them in one-pound boxes, as well as the three-pound boxes." All along, she kept her eye on the other cus-tomer.

Again, this other customer intruded with some more

unsolicited advice, "But I recommend you take the one-pound box of the Colonial. It has creams in it, too!" The clerk on the other side of the counter added, "Yes, why don't you take the one with the creams? The Colonial is really a very nice assortment."

I thought to myself, "Who is working for whom around here?" It really was becoming quite exasperating. "How much is the Colonial box?" I queried. The clerk told me how much it was, and before I could place my order, the customer piped up again and said, "Really, their Colonial box has everything in it. It has chocolate-covered turtles, chocolate-covered cashews, and some nice caramels." Then she added enthusiastically, "And they are in a beautiful package, too!" Just then, she looked at her watch and said, "Oh, I've got to go or I'll miss my plane," and she picked up her bag and left. Both the clerk and I breathed a sigh of relief to see her leave.

Immediately, the clerk turned around and called out, "It's okay, girls, you can come out now. Fannie Mae is gone!" "You're kidding," I gasped. "Oh, no," the clerk replied, "that's Fannie Mae. Well, that's not her real name, of course, but that's her. When her husband died, he left her a candy store. She decided to make something out of her life, and so she put together some new recipes and packaged some new candies, and today she has over a hundred stores all up and down the United States! She calls them her children, and all she does is fly around and visit the different stores."

*She was the authority,* and I didn't even listen to her! She knew the recipes; she put the whole thing together; and I foolishly looked to some clerk as the authority—a clerk who probably never baked her own chocolate in her life!

If you want to know about love, then listen to the real authority on the subject—Jesus Christ! Ministers, priests and psychologists are at best only clerks. We can only take the concept and give it to you. But we don't manufacture it! We don't create it. All the while, maybe through sermons, songs or books, Jesus Christ is coming to you, and you consider Him to be the intruder. You feel vastly relieved when He gets out and lets you alone. But He is the authority! He is perfect love! And "perfect love casts out fear!"

In other words, when Jesus Christ comes into your life, I don't have to tell you what love is. You will know from personal experience! And that's the only way to really know anything. There is a hymn that closes with the words,

"The love of Jesus, what it is,
None but His loved ones know."

It's not something you can be taught; it has to be caught!

# 4

## *The Success Of Love*

Frank Laubach taught me a lesson about love that I've never forgotten. He was talking about perfect love and the fact that none of us love perfectly. Only Christ loves perfectly. No human being is totally perfect in love.

Now let's suppose you run into somebody you can't love. You've tried to love, but you just can't. What do you do? Do you let yourself hate them? No. Do you tell yourself, "I'm a Christian, therefore I'm going to love them." Yes, you tell yourself that, but only telling yourself that might not be enough. So be realistic, what can you do? Surrender to your negative thoughts about that person? Of course not. You call in the expert, the only authority, Jesus Christ.

Here's how Dr. Laubach taught us to handle these situations. First, you put one hand up in the air, open your palm as if you were trying to catch a ball being dropped from above. Then reach out with the other hand and point a finger in the direction of your adversary. Now pray, "Jesus Christ, you are perfect love. I am only imperfect love. Because I'm imperfect, I can't love that person. (Keep your finger pointed right at that person, Laubach would remind us. Point at the heart or at the head.) Jesus Christ, will you please fall into the palm of my hand, flow down through my arm, through my elbow, through my shoulder, my chest, my heart, down my other arm, out of the end of my finger, and will *you* hit this other person, please!?! Hit hard! Hit gently! Hit beautifully with your love. You love that person, Jesus! You can do it, even when I can't. You do it through me!"

I gave that lesson some time ago in this church. One man in the audience thought to himself, "Boy, Schuller's getting carried away again." But a week later, he said to me, "Dr. Schuller, guess what happened? Monday morning I went to work remembering your sermon from the day before. The first person I saw coming into my store was the one salesman I could not stand! I saw him drive up to the curb; I know his car. Before I even saw him get out of the car, I was in a bad mood.

"My secretary, who also attends our church heard the same sermon. She said to me, 'Maybe you'd better try what Dr. Schuller suggested yesterday. Shoot him with love prayers.' So before he came into the store, I reached one hand up into the air and pointed the other hand at him through the window. He was gawking at me as if I was nuts. But I prayed, 'Jesus, I can't love that guy, I can't even stomach him to say nothing about loving him. But you can. Flow into my hand, through my arm, through my heart, and You love him, Jesus.'

"And the most amazing thing happened. I couldn't believe it. When the man came up to me he said, 'Good morning. How are you today?' And I've never heard him say it that way before. I looked at his face and saw that his countenance looked different than I had ever seen him before. His eyes, which always looked so nasty, looked sweet. It worked! I ended up loving this guy!"

*"Perfect love casts out fear."* It casts out all kinds of negative forces. Perfect love is Christ flowing through you. Christ is the perfect love. So the secret, of course, is to have a personal relationship with Jesus Christ. And this is possible!

Why does perfect love cast out fear? For one simple reason: Selfish love always produces fear. If I love you because I need you or because I want you, I'll always be afraid that I might not get you. And then I'll have lost something that I wanted to gain. But if I love because I want to give something to someone, I'll never become fearful or worried or tense. For a giving love can never lose! If the other person likes what is offered, you succeed! Either way, you can't lose. So there will be no subliminal anxieties or fears of being rejected or hurt. *Selfish love is the kind of love that builds walls, not bridges.*

About a month ago I was in St. Louis, Missouri, where I was to give a lecture. It was four o'clock in the afternoon, and I was to give my lecture in the main hall that night. As I unpacked my suitcase, I pulled out my grey suit that I was going to wear for my lecture, just to make sure it was in good shape. Then I made this discovery: I hadn't worn the suit for four months and in the meantime I had lost 36 pounds. So the trousers were way too big for me. Unfortunately, it was one of those styles of pants that didn't have belt loops.

Now you talk about being nervous! To be a lecturer on a platform in a pair of pants that are a 42 when you now wear a size 37—I had a problem! I knew I either had to get a very hefty safety pin or I needed some emergency tailoring done in a hurry. I called the desk in the hotel. They told me no tailor could do it in such a short time. But they said, "You can always go to Mr. Harris. Maybe he could do it."

So I went down to Harris the Tailor in the mall in downtown St. Louis, three blocks away. There I met one of the most marvelous men. Mr. Harris was a seasoned gentleman, who really knew his business. "Sir, can you take my trousers in about four inches?" I asked. "Well, that'll take about two hours," he answered. I looked him right in the eyeballs and asked, "Sir, aren't you Mr. Harris?" "Yes," he answered. I continued. "Well, I was told you're the best tailor in town." "Well, ah . . . ," he hesitated. I went on, "I happen to know a tailor in Los Angeles that could do it in twenty minutes. And I'm sure you're better than he is." He just stared at me. And I stared back at him, because I needed the job done. He finally said, "Okay, go to that little room there and throw me your trousers."

I walked into the room, carrying a book I had just bought, when Mr. Harris asked, "What's the name of that book you've got?" "*Loneliness, the Fear of Love*," I told him. "Well, you're going to get awful lonely in there waiting for these pants to get done," he said. "Oh, I don't think I'll get lonely," I replied. "I never get lonely, because I've got a friend who is with me."

Seventeen minutes later my trousers were back with the best job of tailoring I've ever seen!!

"Are you a minister or something?" Mr. Harris asked me as he handed me my trousers. "You look a little familiar." "Yes, sir, I am," I told him. "What kind of religion do you have. What is your faith?" he asked. "I'm glad you asked that, Mr. Harris," I said. "What kind of faith do I have? Well, it's not a *religion*. By that I mean simply a course like sociology, anthropology, biology or like chemistry. It's not a religion like some spiritual kind of philosophy. And it's not a set of *restrictions*. 'Don't do this, don't do that.' It's not a list of *resolutions*: 'I'm going to do this, I'm going to do that.' And it's not a *ritual*: 'Now we pray, now we bow our heads, now we give the offering. Now we read the Bible.' No, my faith is a *relationship!* I have a friend, and his name is Jesus Christ! I have received Him into my life, and I feel that within me there is a love that will never leave me. There is a love that gives me the power to conquer my fears. I'm not afraid even to die, because I know that I won't go to hell, I'll go to heaven. I have a Savior, so all my ultimate fears are flushed out. My friend died on a cross for me and He has the scars to prove His love for me!"

Do you want to succeed? Have you discovered the dynamic force for success in your life? I invite you now to receive Jesus Christ into your life by faith. When He comes in, then a Love will come into your life that will give you an amazing peace of mind! You will discover the ability to speak the language of love—I forgive.

You will find the power to live fearlessly. And you will see possibilities in situations that before you have always considered hopeless!

Choose love! By choosing love, you will be choosing to receive Jesus Christ into your life, right now!

# Discover
## The Power For
## Overcoming Defeat

# 1

## Relief From Depression

I suppose no particular mood characterizes our country today more than the mood of vague depression. I come to you today as a spokesman for God to say to you, be of good cheer! There is hope! *Gloom can be doomed!*

There is a cure for depression. What we have to learn, of course, is some basic things that we will never learn from secular society. We must understand that there is such a problem called sin in the human heart.

I do a lot of travelling around the country, and I have detected an enormous mood of gloom in our nation. There is a real epidemic of depression. And the country doesn't seem to have an antidote for it. In the United States, we have built a civilization on the belief that you can educate gloom out of people. And if you are unable to educate success and happiness, then you can legislate it. Somehow, we have developed the idea that through education, legislation or organization, we can come to know and experience a full and complete life.

No one is ever going to have a joyful, fulfilled life through education alone, through legislation alone, through organization alone, not even through prescriptions. Yes, there are those who, in a period of gloom, think they can find joy in a box of pills or a bottle. But if history has proven anything in the last few years it is this: All the education, all the legislation, all the organization, all the prescriptions and all the doctors and pharmaceutical companies in the world cannot give to you what you really need in order to have joy within yourself. St. Augustine put it right when he said, "Our souls are restless, O Lord, until they rest in Thee." We human beings, by nature, are detached from God. And, detached from God, we are like a tree that has been cut; the roots do not support us with nourishment. When you are really connected to God, you have His spirit flowing into you.

And the spirit of God is the spirit of hope!
The spirit of God is the spirit of love!
The spirit of God is the spirit of joy!
The spirit of God is the spirit of faith!
The spirit of God is the spirit of optimism!
The spirit of God is the spirit of confidence!
The spirit of God is the spirit of courage!

Now if you don't have these tremendous emotions surging through you, it means that something is blocking the flow of God into your life, and that blockage we call *sin*. You're not going to cure it through education, legislation or organization. And you will not ultimately correct it with a pill, a bottle, a box or a bag of marijuana. The cure for the soul is spiritual! To begin with, what you need to do is to think positively. Be a possibility thinker, and see how your soul can be saved.

Our first home in California was on a lot that was eighty feet wide. When we bought that home I noticed that between the curb and the sidewalk there was this vast piece of ground. Ten feet wide and eighty feet long. "What can I plant there?" I thought. "If I plant grass or flowers, people will step out of their cars on to it, and it will be crushed." Then I had a bright idea. "I'll just take out some of the dirt, put in sand and fill it with bricks." All I would have to do was dig out about eight inches of dirt from this ten foot by eighty foot strip of land.

So one Monday morning, with great enthusiasm, I got out there with my wheelbarrow and my shovel. I excavated a hole about twelve inches by twelve inches and eight inches deep. And I looked at the wheelbarrow, and by this time, it was already half full.

Just then, one of my neighbors was leaving for work. He stopped because he was surprised to see me out there with a wheelbarrow and a shovel. "What are you doing?" he asked. "Well, I'm going to take the dirt out the whole distance of this strip, and I'm going to fill it with sand and gravel and bricks," was my answer. Then he asked me something that I had never thought about: "What are you going to do with all the ground?" "Well," I said, with a flash of inspiration, "I think I'll make a little mound in the backyard." "You're going to have a big mound," he warned me, "an awful lot of dirt is going to come out of that hole. You know, that's going to take you a few weeks before you can get that all shoveled out."

I enthused, "Look, all I have to do is practice possibility thinking, and it'll be out in no time!" With that, my neighbor left for work.

I finished filling the wheelbarrow full of dirt and

hauled it to the backyard. Already, I had a bigger mound than I needed. And I had only taken out an area about a foot and a half square!

By this time it was nine o'clock, and I was sweating. Quite reverently I said, "Lord, there must be a better way to do this!" Five minutes later a member of my church came driving down the street with his dump truck, and on his dump truck he had a little tractor. Mounted on the front of the tractor he had a skip loader. "Reverend, what are you doing?" Roy questioned as he pulled to the curb. I told him and then asked, "What are you doing here?" And he replied, "I'm lost." "Oh no, you're not lost!" I said. "God found you!" He looked at my project and suddenly said, "You know, I could do that job for you in thirty minutes and I need the dirt!" He dropped the gate on his truck, brought his tractor down, rolled up to the curb, dug into that ground, and by 11:30 the job was finished and he was gone.

My neighbor came home for lunch at noon, and I was sweeping up the dust! He is a possibility thinker today!

Really, if you think you have a problem, I want you to know that God has an answer for it. A problem of gloom and doom is sweeping our country today. What we haven't realized is that we're paying the high cost of being lost. And the high cost of being lost is to be cut off from the source of our inspiration and spiritual power.

What gets people depressed anyway? We say, of course, it's sin that blocks God's healing flow of positive emotion power into your life. When that happens, a man becomes a lost soul. *And a lost soul is a deflated and defeated soul. And that's what gets people depressed.*

I don't think anything illustrates this more than the story of the prodigal son, a beautiful story that Jesus tells.

He was a young man, not unlike most single young men and women of our own day—very up-to-date.

If you're a single, excited, young person, my advice to you is to develop a philosophy of life, a code of values and morals, so you can go places without going to pieces.

This young guy went places, but he also went to pieces. He took his inheritance early, cashed it in, then went out and spent it on girls and everything else. Before he realized it, his cash was gone. As a result, he entered into a period of real depression.

Depression, psychologists now tell us, is caused primarily by two things. I summarize it by saying that depression is caused by being deflated or defeated. The prodigal son was deflated. He found himself, of all places, in the swine pen with the pigs, and with his money gone. I think the most tragic sentence he uttered in that place is the sentence that many people utter, even though they don't reach that low state. He said, "I am unworthy to be called my father's son." *I am unworthy!*

I wrote a book some years ago, entitled, *Self-Love, The Dynamic Force of Success*. In it I verbalized what I believe Jesus Christ teaches, and that is this: Self-love is the ultimate human value. If you have a great sense of self-dignity, self-esteem and self-worth, wow!

What does it mean to be a lost soul? It means to be deflated. "I'm nobody. I'm nothing. I don't count. I don't matter." A lost soul forgets who he or she is.

What we really have is a self-love crisis. Of course, there are lots of people who don't know who they are. But their identity crisis is caused by a self-esteem crisis. They don't dare to find out who they are. They are afraid that if they uncover their real self, they will be ashamed and embarrassed by what they would find. Most people with an identity crisis really suffer from a self-love crisis. And to be deflated is to be depressed.

No college classroom has an answer to that problem. No state or national legislature can pass a law to cure that deflated feeling. Ultimately then, how do you overcome that deflated, self-degrading feeling that comes over you? The only way is to experience acceptance by someone you look up to as a beautiful ideal person. Wow! That will really make you feel like you're somebody again. And you need to remember who you are. If you are feeling deflated and think you're a nothing and don't matter; when you don't have connections, wealth, power or position; when you don't know any important people and feel you are a nobody, remember this: *You are a child of God!* And that's somebody! Remember who you are!

The tragic thing is, when a deflated person doesn't love himself, he loses moral motivation! And that usually makes a person feel even worse about himself. So a negative self-image feeds upon itself. The cure is to discover your divine heritage.

Legend tells us that the beautiful Helen of Troy, over whom many wars were fought, was lost following one of the battles. When the army returned to Greece, Helen was not on any of the ships. Menelaus went to try to find her, at great personal peril. Finally, in one of the seaport villages, he found her. She had been wounded and was suffering from amnesia. Forgetting who she was, she stooped to the level of the women in the streets, making her living as a prostitute.

When Menelaus found her, she was in rags covered with dirt. In her shame and dishonor, he looked upon her. Finally, he called out, "Helen." Her head turned. "You are Helen of Troy!" he said. And her back straightened and the royal look returned as she heard those words. She was redeemed!

You may be deflated and dishonored in your own eyes because you don't realize who you are. *You are a member of the royal family.* When you accept Jesus Christ into your life, you are a member of the family of God. You are no longer a lost soul. You are no longer deflated. You have been forgiven and have recovered your honor!

When the prodigal son returned home, his father was so glad to see him that he did two things: First, he brought out a beautiful robe and put it over his son's shoulders. Then he brought out a ring to put on his son's finger—dramatizing his son's moment of honor restored. Depression comes when you're deflated. Joy comes when you are restored and uplifted!

The second mark of a lost soul is that he is not only deflated, he's defeated. A deflated soul becomes a defeated soul when he doesn't love himself. Not only does this person lose moral motivation, he or she also loses the motivation to achieve and to succeed. The one who says, "I can do nothing" thinks he or she is a nobody.

Now a great change comes into your life when Jesus Christ saves you from your guilt and self-condemnation. The Deliverer delivers you from your tendency to put yourself down. Here's what happens: Jesus Christ becomes the new core of your life! When God is inside of you, you'll know it. Then you can say with St. Paul, *"I can do all things through Christ who strengthens me"* (Philippians 4:13).

Now that's why people who are lost and then saved are able to break habits that medicine alone has been unable to permanently break. I'm talking about heroin addiction. In the whole drug problem no one has had a better success rate of healing heroin addicts than Jesus Christ! And that's a fact!

Depressed? Are you hooked on a habit? A habit that you can't get over? Maybe it's eating too much of the wrong foods. Maybe it's drinking too much. Maybe it's smoking too much. Do you think it's hopeless? Is it driving you up the wall? God can change you!

On our church property we have walnut trees, and in the fall the walnut trees drop their leaves. In the winter, we have what we call in California the Santa Ana winds. These strong winds come and blow the leaves off. I was walking through the barren grove the other day, and I saw here and there a dead leaf still clinging to a branch. The winds hadn't blown them off, and the storms had not washed them off.

You may have a problem like that. Winds will not blow it off. Storms will not wash it off. It's hopeless? No, it's not! You just wait. In a little while, new sap

will come from deep roots, surging through the trunk, into the branches and a new bud will push the dead leaf off. *Every dead leaf that still clings in the wintertime is doomed, because new life will push it off.*

Depressed? Deflated? Defeated? New life can come in you! How do you get it? You get it by admitting you need help. That's the key; you can't do it alone. Jesus said, *"I am the vine, you are the branches. He who abides in me, and I in him, he it is that bears much fruit, for apart from me you can do nothing"* (John 15:5).

You must be grafted into Jesus Christ. Do like that prodigal son did. Be humble enough to know and to admit that there is help at home.

G.K. Chesterton said, "There are two ways to get home. One way is to stay there and never leave; the second way is to keep going until you get back."

Some of you are at home with God even though you never really felt Him. You were born in a Christian family; you were nurtured in the Christian vein. You became a Christian just as naturally as you came into this world through the womb of your mother, and that's the natural way.

Jesus said, *"Whoever does not receive the kingdom of God like a child shall not enter it."* What Jesus meant is that normally conversion should be a very natural thing. So you grew up in a Christian home, you met Jesus Christ through your parents, and you had a second birth somewhere along the line as natural as the first birth. You became like a child who grows or like a flower that grows. You unfolded into a beautiful Christian. You are at home; you never left it.

But some of you are not at home with God. You're trying everything to find cures for depression, but you have never yet tried Jesus Christ. Some of you do not have Christian fathers and mothers. Or if you had Christian parents, you drifted and you left God and you left home. The way for you to get home is to go back home. And you are doing that now.

Deflated? Come back. You *are* somebody. God thinks you're great. Your life is going to change. You know, the cynic says, "You can't change human nature." And I say, the cynic is right. You can't change human nature, *but God can!*

Defeated? The prodigal son was defeated. If there is anything that depresses a person more than a lack of self-esteem it is a feeling of helplessness, inability to cope, inability to succeed—the consciousness of being a failure.

G. K. Chesterton tells the story of two men who were dissatisfied with England. They got on a boat and went off into the fog on what they thought was a far-off journey. Finally, one day, out of the fog an island emerged, and they went ashore. They stepped aground and said, "What a beautiful island. We will make this our home." A stranger came by, and they asked, "We've just landed here. Can you tell us where we are?" And the man said, "You are on the north coast of England." They had come back home.

There is only one hope for your joyful living—try Jesus. He'll come and save you from your deflated and defeated feeling. He'll deliver you. You'll get a new passion within the core of your being. You'll have an integrating force. You'll have a hub that holds all the spokes together. What you have to do is admit you need help and then accept the help that He wants to give.

You can move from *swineland* to *shineland*, from *despair* to *hope*, from *gloom* to *joy*, if you'll simply come back home to God.

# 2

# New Hope
# For Troubled People

If the cup of your heart is a little empty and needs an infilling of hope, courage, joy and inner strength, God can fill it! I have new hope for troubled people today.

Obviously, one of the biggest problems in human existence is to distinguish between authentic needs and wants. Robert Arday, the anthropologist, wrote a book some years ago called, *The Territorial Imperative*, in which he said that every man needs three things—he needs identity, he needs stimulation, and he needs security. He went on to explain, "There's really only one way that these three needs can be met sociologically, and that's through war. In a nationalistic war, a person knows who he is. 'I am a German,' or 'I am a Russian,' or 'I am an American.' So he has a sense of identity in battle. At the same time, he had stimulation—there's no boredom in wartime. And there is the development of security, for the purpose of a war is to provide security for the wife and children."

I have good news for you! I know a way that is better than warfare to meet these three needs. They can be met when the human being experiences what Jesus Christ called *salvation*.

Have you ever had someone come up to you on the sidewalk and almost knock you into the street, while enthusiastically, saying, "Brother, are you saved?" Wow, that can really scare you, can't it? In the past, I think the word *saved*—even the word *lost*—has been vulgarized by sincere, well-meaning people. And nothing is more tragic than when a great word is politicized, plagiarized or vulgarized to the point that the word immediately turns people off.

But I want to add that if you read your New Testament, and you read the story of Jesus, you'll see that this word *saved* comes up again and again. So it's very important for us to understand what the word means.

Now think of this: The image Jesus wanted to create in His community was not the image of a high-powered executive, not a VIP, not a big wheel, not even that of a friend of the powerful politicians. Oddly enough, He wanted to project the image of a shepherd!

This may be very hard to understand, unless you've been to the Holy Land. If you've been to Israel, you know something about the shepherd, who was one of the lowly people during Jesus' day, and still is one of the common folk. Imagine: the shepherd is alone out there on the hillsides with his sheep in the heat of the summer sun without shade, and in the cold winter nights. The shepherd—lonely, dedicated, committed, caring—loving the helpless sheep. The shepherd, with

his leathery rawhide-tanned skin, his narrow squinting eyes constantly scanning the hills, the ravines, the rocks and the brush to be sure that every one of his sheep are there. When the shepherd sees that one is missing, he will go out and look until he finds it. Then he picks it up and literally puts it around his shoulders, carrying it back to the sheepfold. The shepherd— this was the image Jesus wanted to project.

Well, it probably isn't so odd when you think that the prophet said, *"He will feed his flock like a shepherd . . . and gently lead those that are with young"* (Isaiah 40:11). And it isn't odd when you think of the fact that in the Jewish community, Jesus, of course, was raised in the Jewish community, the 23rd Psalm was a familiar one: *"The Lord is my shepherd, I shall not want; he makes me lie down in green pastures."*

But in the Gospel of St. John, Chapter 10, Jesus is saying,

"I am the good shepherd . . . I say to you, he who does not enter the sheepfold by the door, but climbs in by another way, that man is a thief and a robber . . . Truly, I say to you, I am the door of the sheep. All who came before me are thieves and robbers; but the sheep did not heed them. I am the door; if any one enters by me, he will be saved, and will go in and out and find pasture. The thief comes only to steal and kill and destroy; I came that they may have life, and have it abundantly. I am the good shepherd. The good shepherd lays down his life for the sheep . . . I am the good shepherd; I know my own and my own know me, as the Father knows me and I know the Father; and I lay down my life for the sheep. And I have other sheep, that are not of this fold; I must bring them also, and they will heed my voice. So there shall be one flock, one shepherd. For this reason the Father loves me, because I lay down my life, that I may take it again. No one takes it from me, but I lay it down of my own accord. I have power to lay it down, and I have power to take it again; this charge I have received from my Father" (John 10:7-12, 14-18).

What does it mean to be saved? I submit, it can mean these three things: identity, stimulation and security.

## Identity

Once you become a member of God's family and you know that you are one of Jesus Christ's friends, you feel like you are a part of a great flock of happy believers. That's identity. "I know who I am. I am a Christian." That's a beautiful feeling.

With this identity comes, naturally, a new birth of self-worth. Too many people do not love themselves. They put themselves down. *You cannot put a price on anything until you first label it.* Mark that well. If you don't know how to label it, how can you ever tell how to price it?

One of the diamonds from the Crown of one of the Kings of Europe was for months in a piazza stall in Rome labeled, "Rock crystal, 1 franc." "Rock crystal" that was sold for one franc! And it turned out to be a diamond of priceless value!

You will sell yourself too cheap, my friend, until you know who you are, until you become a part of the family of God. That's identity. Then you are somebody.

We speak of people being saved, for they know who they are. They're Christians; they're children of God. We speak of other people as being lost. They are lost because they don't know where they came from or who they are.

I remember a tense experience a couple of years ago that happened about a mile from our church. As I approached the stop light, I saw, toddling in the middle of the intersection, a little girl about two years old. I screeched my car to a stop at the light and got out. At the same time cars were coming from every direction, and they stopped, too. Here was a little toddler in the middle of the intersection, like a confused puppy dog. We met in the middle of the intersection. We looked at this little girl and didn't quite know what to do. Finally, one of the gentlemen reached out and she took hold of his big finger, and we all walked to the side of the street.

"What's your name?" we asked. "Mary," she answered. "Mary what?" "Hmmm?" "What's your name, Mary?" we asked again. "Hmmm?" "Where do you live, Mary?" "I don't know." "Do you live in that direction?" we pressed. "I don't know." "This way?" "I don't know." "That way?" "I don't know."

Our conversation was not producing any results. Fortunately someone came along the sidewalk about that time and said, "You know, I think I've seen this little girl before. I've seen her toddle out in the street over there, down the way a bit. I'll take her down there and see if she'll recognize her place." And so he left with Mary.

I knew the fellow, so when I met him later I asked, "Whatever happened to little Mary?" "Oh," he replied, "I took her down the street and over two blocks. As soon as she got there, she let go of my hand and started running. She knew where she was. She recognized the street and her house."

Now it's bad enough to be lost, but if you're lost and don't know your address, you're in trouble. And there

are many people who are lost in life and don't know their address. They don't know where they came from or where their home is. They have forgotten completely that they are descendants of God!

You know, when you start getting close to God, that's like recognizing your own street. And when you get close to Jesus Christ, it's like feeling the vibration of the house where you belong. You feel at home. You feel a deep peace within yourself. Knowing where you belong is like the salmon, who instinctively return upstream to the waters of their origin. Or like the hummingbird who crosses the waters of the Gulf in the winter to return to California's warm climate. There is an inner instinct within you that lets you know you are home where you belong. You've been saved!

Identity—You'll find out who you are. You're not just an evolved ape, you are a descendant of God.

To be saved means to be adopted into God's family. Wherever you are now, God invites you to be a member of His family, and this happens by an act of faith, by letting God love you.

You know, you are a creature designed to be a believer. The man who has faith is the one who is healthy. The man who is doubtful and cynical is the one who is unhealthy. You can prove it scientifically. A person who is a believer is a joyous, relaxed, emotionally mature, healthy human being. But a doubter and a cynic is uptight. He becomes suspicious, quarrelsome, debatable, controversial, argumentative, cold, cool, and he withdraws. He is not a wholesome, healthy, happy personality.

Man was born and designed to be at his healthiest when he is believing. Faith is the natural air that man was meant to breathe. Let yourself go! Let God love you! Let yourself be a believer! Quit fighting it! He loves you, no matter who you are, no matter what you've done!

I recall reading a story about a minister in a midwestern city. This minister had one son who became a close friend of a professional man in the community who was a professed atheist, a man who drank too much, a man who paid no attention to the Ten Commandments. The boy became such a close friend of this professional until he, too, was drinking too much and wasting his life and his substance. He wouldn't even communicate after awhile to his father and mother. One night, his father woke up and his wife was not in bed. He got up, wondering where she was. He walked around, and then looked in his son's room. There he saw his wife, kneeling at her son's bedside, kissing his hand. The boy lay there sleeping, stone drunk. She lifted her head, turned to her husband and with tears in her eyes said, "He won't let me love him when he's awake."

Let God love you. That's your natural way of living. Let Christ come in while you're wide awake!

Identity—you'll know who you are from then on. You are a child of God!

## Stimulation

Now enjoy the stimulation of the group. Man is a gregarious creature, designed to live in groups. We need our solitude, but we cannot survive in total individuality. We need the stimulation of other minds and other personalities.

What's the terrible thing about loneliness? It's boredom, that's what. I know lots of people who live in solitude. They are not married; they are single. Some have lost a husband; others have lost a wife. They live alone, but they are not lonely because they are so excited about projects they are working on, and about their involvement in the church, in the community and in their work. We need interrelationships with other persons for stimulation.

Join God's group and you'll be stimulated to dream dreams and to amount to something! Everybody I have ever known, when they were truly *saved*, that was the time they started to relate to the group and to dream great dreams! They started to grow—to become somebody!

What happens when you become a Christian? You are brought into the flock. When you're brought into the flock, you hear the voice of the shepherd say to you, "You can be more than you have been. God has better plans for you." And you get stimulated.

Stimulation—you get it in Christianity.

### Security

That's the last thing you've got when you are saved by Jesus Christ. You have security in the here and now.

I've had letters recently from people who have seen a movie that's been going around dramatizing the work of the devil. And no small amount of psychological damage has been done by that film, incidentally. I keep reading this verse to these people:

> "Christ has delivered us from the dominion of darkness and transferred us to the kingdom of his beloved Son" (Colossians 1:13).

Wow! There are all kinds of negative forces, negative thinkers, negative powers and negative vibrations in this world around us, and He saves us from them! He does, right here and now. And He saves us for eternity.

Concentrate on the positive. If you accept Jesus Christ as your Savior and take Him in your life, you'll never have to worry about the devil. In Colossians 1:12 Paul sums it up so beautifully: *"Give thanks to the Father, who has qualified us to share in the inheritance of the saints in light."*

### Security in the
### Face of Eternity

I remember when my Dad, at eighty-two years old, wasn't feeling well and had to go to the hospital. Mom said he packed his suitcase with his stiff old hands and walked to the front door. Then he looked back and she said he looked at the whole living room. He looked at the ceiling, the walls, the pictures, and then he looked at the old chair where he always sat. He smiled a little and said, "Well, Jenny, let's go. I won't be coming back here again." And she said that he said it like somebody about to graduate, ready to walk across the stage to get his diploma. Like somebody who was going home! He was proud of the life he had lived! He left for the hospital—and passed away there a few days later.

To be saved means that you come to the end—*very confident!* Identity, stimulation, security—they're your gifts. All you have to do is take them and say, "Thank you, Lord."

Take these gifts and enjoy the JOY of being saved!

# *Discover Your Opportunities*

# 1

## Four Approaches
## To Problems

I want you to consider with me your problems, because you can never reach out in life without running into problems. And it is very important that you develop a positive attitude toward problems.

What I want to say is built on the confidence expressed by St. Paul, when he wrote,

> "For I am persuaded, that neither death, nor life, nor angels, nor principalities, nor powers, nor things present, nor things to come, nor height, nor depth, nor any other creature, shall be able to separate us from the love of God, which is in Christ Jesus our Lord."
>
> (Romans 8:38 , 39)

Let me suggest four attitudinal philosophies toward problems. Two are positive and two are negative. This means you have four choices when you run into any problem. Your first choice is to simply *consent* to it. Your second choice is to *resent* it. Your third choice is to *invent* a solution. And your fourth possibility is to *prevent* the problem from getting worse and from coming back at you later.

1. When a problem hits you, you can simply decide to *consent* to it—give up, quit, accept defeat.

I was on a television program recently in Pittsburgh, Pa. It was one of those shows where people can call in with questions after you are interviewed. One of my Hour of Power viewers from the city called and said, "Dr. Schuller, I've been listening to you and I am convinced that I should pray and practice possibility thinking. But, Dr. Schuller, what do you do when you pray and pray and practice positive thinking over and over again and the problems still don't go away?"

I answered, "At that time you consider your only two alternatives: one alternative is to give in, quit praying and quit practicing positive thinking and be a total negative thinker. I can tell you what will happen if you do that. Everything will get darker and your road ahead will be paved with catastrophe. The will to die will be so strong that you will want to commit suicide. Now, that's one alternative.

"If you have been praying and practicing positive thinking and you still are in as bad a strait as you were and things are no better, all I can say is that it has worked. For life would have been much worse than it is. You can take the one alternative to quit or you can choose the other alternative, and this is, keep right on keeping on, thinking positively and praying positively."

"But," she continued, "what if things still don't change?" And I replied, "If you keep on keeping on and the situation doesn't change, at least you will have become a more beautiful person for those who have to put up with you in the process. So what are your alternatives but to keep on keeping on?"

In facing a problem, your first option is to *consent* to it, surrender and give in to it. But that is a poor choice because of what it does to you. You are defeated.

2. The second option in facing a problem is to *resent* it.

Lots of people choose that reaction. You can *resent* it and you will become tough, hard, cold and bitter. You'll feel sorry for yourself. You'll think the world is against you, God has abandoned you, your friends don't understand you and people don't love you. And then you'll really be where anybody with self-pity lands up—at the end of the road, lonely, isolated and unloved. The reason you will not be surrounded by love is because you, in your self-pity, will have driven your friends away from you.

I had a ride in a cab the other day in Washington with a cab driver who was taking me and my producer back to the airport. He was really a hard, cold, bitter and cynical man. In fact, I couldn't even begin to use the language he used. He was really rough and obscene. He didn't know I was a minister. Directing the conversation to the realm of religion, I finally said to him, "Are you a Christian?" He said, "Sure." "What kind?" I questioned. "A real one or a hypocrite?" He answered, "Well, I guess I'm a real one." He was so tough and so bitter because his first marriage hadn't panned out and his second marriage didn't work out either. Then he had been living with a woman for four years and he finally told her to get out. He was simply a man who had become very miserable and was now nearing sixty years of age.

There was one basic reason why he had turned into the kind of person he was—all his life he developed an attitude of resentment. *When problems hit him, he got mad*. That came through very clear! I didn't have to ride in that cab for very long before I could see that here was a man who started a style of living forty years before at the age of twenty. He had gotten into the rut of always reacting to problems by getting mad.

Now you can resent problems and turn into a resentful and resented kind of a person! But this man was so miserable that I did something I seldom do: I said to him, "If you think you are a Christian, let me ask you a question. If you died tonight would you go to heaven or would you go to hell?" "I'm not sure," he answered. I said, "Well, I can tell you how to be sure." He looked in the mirror and asked, "What do you do anyway?" I told him, "I write books and I'm a minister and I can tell you how to be sure. What you have to do is get Jesus Christ into your life, my friend. Jesus promised, *'Him that cometh to me I will in no wise cast out'* (John 6:37). What you have to do is come to Jesus Christ and admit that you have sinned. Your negative thinking is the worst kind of a sin you could commit." He looked up in the mirror and I looked at him.

As the taxi reached the air terminal, I said to the driver, "Just sit tight. Keep the car running if you want to, but I'm going to let you have an opportunity right now to become an authentic Christian. An authentic Christian is not somebody who goes griping through life but he is one who accepts Jesus Christ as his Savior." Then I led him in a little prayer. He claimed to have accepted Jesus Christ and I believe he did. I said to him, "Now if tonight by some chance you should suddenly find yourself facing the Almighty God at the door of heaven, whatever you do, don't rattle off a long list of the good things you have done in life. He will not be impressed. Instead, you are to give a call for Jesus and just remind Him what He promised you. He is a Man of His Word. He has promised that if any man comes unto Him, He will never cast him out. You know, you are a different man than you were ten minutes ago." And by now he really was.

I was looking into the face of a man whose countenance had changed. He was radiant. He was calm. He was tranquil. The skin, instead of being uptight, tense and angry, was absolutely radiating warmth. He looked like he had love inside of him. And he did. He was a different person because a different Spirit had come into his life. It was Jesus Christ.

So face your problems. It doesn't make sense to resent them or consent to them because that will only turn you into a miserable person.

3. Your third option is to *invent* solutions. Make sure Jesus Christ is in your life, in which case, you will have His Holy Spirit to guide you and direct you. Romans 8:28 says, *"All things work together for good to them that love God, to them who are the called according to his purpose."* Many people have twisted that Bible verse to give the impression that God deliberately inflicts all these problems upon you for your own good. That is not what the Bible says.

Inventing solutions is what we mean by possibility thinking. You see, we believe that if God allows a problem to come to us, it doesn't mean He wanted us to have it necessarily in the first place. It is not God's will for many of these problems to come to us. But He allows them to come because He's allowed us to have free will. You know that when God made you, He had a choice. He could either make a puppet or a person, a human being or a perfect computer. A perfect computer brings no glory to God. A puppet is no glory to its manipulator. But a person and a human being who has freedom to say "yes" or "no" is the only kind of person who can glorify God. *Love is meaningless unless you have the freedom not to love.* "Yes" has no meaning unless you have the freedom to say "no." And that is why if you were a beautiful computer you would be no glory to God.

God made us with a free will, and most of the problems that hit us in one way or another stem back to our own mistakes or the sins of other people, but they are not God's fault. When they come, He makes it possible for us to invent solutions and turns the difficulty into dividends, the problems into opportunities, the cross into a crown and Good Friday into an Easter. The thorns of our Lord can become the stars in His crown!

This is the option you have. Look for the possibilities in the problem.

I love people who make creative solutions to problems. I read recently about a railroad express clerk near Redwood Falls, Minnesota, whose last name was Sears. One day, somebody sent him a whole box of watches to be delivered to the jeweler in town. But the jeweler didn't want the box of watches. So Sears wrote back to the Chicago distributor and asked, "What shall I do with them?" The distributor in Chicago said, "Well, I don't know what to do with them. The postage is too expensive. You can go ahead and have them for a few bucks a piece if you want them." So the railroad clerk turned his problem into an opportunity. He invented a creative, redemptive solution. He simply put together a catalog, drew some pictures, sent them to all the other railroad clerks, and they bought his watches. It was so successful he ordered more watches and enlarged his catalog. You know it today as the Sears, Roebuck catalog.

One of my favorite stories is that of the beautiful artist, Sir Edwin Landseer, a famous artist of animals. One of his greatest paintings is in Scotland. It is on the wall of a beautiful inn that overlooks the rugged terrain. Some years back during a celebration when the inn was new, somebody popped open a bottle of soda and it sprayed on the newly painted wall before the paint and plaster were dry. It left dirty brown stains running down to the floor. It was very embarrassing. The host who owned the place became very irate and understandably so. He made a scene and evicted the drunken guest. The party broke up early.

One of the guests was Sir Edwin. After everyone had left, including the host, he locked the door, flipped on a light, opened his bag, took out his paint and brushes and soon the big brown stain was turned into a brown rock. Then he painted cypress, evergreen, spruce and the rest of the mountainside. And on the rock, standing on two feet, was a picture you may have seen reproduced as the Mountain Stag, a goat with his horns curled, standing like a proud beast. And curling around the rock was a mountain stream with white foam. He turned an ugly stain into a beautiful painting. He turned an obstacle into an opportunity.

Carl Jung, the esteemed Swiss psychiatrist of a generation back, said, "Among all of my patients over 35, there has not been one whose problem in the last resort was not that of finding a religious outlook on life. And none of them, I repeat, none of them, were ever healed who did not regain a religious outlook on life."

Some of you will never have the power to invent solutions and overcome the temptation to consent to or resent problems until you have the belief that God has control of your life and that He is planning it in such a way that even this dark time can be turned into a beautiful scene.

I'll tell you why I'm a possibility thinker—I know I am not riding alone. I know that God is my friend. His presence with me makes me a Possibility Thinker!

4. Your fourth option in facing a problem is to *prevent* it from ever recurring again. Learn from your mistakes. Learn from your difficulties. So many of the problems that come to us come because we violate natural laws. We don't eat right. We don't exercise right. We don't sleep right. We drink or smoke too much. When you don't take care of your body, you become sick. It's inevitable that you're going to have problems. You can't escape it. Age is inevitable and if you don't take care of your body you're going to have problems. You neglect natural law.

Some of you have problems because you neglect spiritual laws. Spiritual laws say that you should feed your mind on God's Word. And some of you haven't gotten into the habit. You come to church once and then maybe a month later or six weeks later. And that's

not enough. The human soul has an inspirational tank that only holds a seven-day supply. And unless you are going downhill, you'll start sputtering pretty soon. Prevent the problems from coming.

There are physical laws, there are spiritual laws and there are moral laws. The Ten Commandments are not respected in our society today. And I don't read them from the pulpit, but believe me, they are the moral law. I don't care who you are, if you decide that you don't have to live by these Ten Commandments and you don't have to live by natural laws, physical laws, or moral laws, you are going to have problems. This is not a threat. It's a warning. A warning is issued in love. A threat is issued in hostility. I love you. And so I must warn you: live by the natural laws, live by the spiritual laws, live by the moral laws and prevent the problems from coming back to you. Then truly if you are in tune with God through Jesus Christ, you can know that He is your friend.

I saw a fantastic musical in Washington, D.C., entitled, "Your Arms Too Short to Box With God." Pontius Pilate is told, "Don't try to fight Jesus. Your arms are too short to box with God."

Some of you have been trying to box with God. If you fight Him, you can't win. Your arms are too short. The only thing to do is to decide today that God is real, and then draw close to Him. And how do you do that? Well, sometimes the idea of God is too big, like a grandiose concept. I've been asked, "Schuller, when you think of God, what do you think in your mind?" *The only way I can get a handle on God is to get a handle on Jesus*.

And that's my advice to you. If you want to get a handle on God, get a handle on Jesus. Jesus Christ is real. Right now, if you invite Him to come into your life, He will do so. There will be a beautiful warm Spirit flooding your mind. There will be a happy sense of peace of mind. It will be the power of the Holy Spirit. This will be the presence of God. It will be your salvation. And with Jesus Christ living within you, you will be able to invent solutions to your problems and prevent them from coming back!

# 2

## *Your Frustrations Can Be Fruitful*

When you seek to invent solutions to your problems, or try to prevent them from coming back to you, you will run into frustrations. But I have some good news for you along with that disturbing bit of information. It is possible for you to draw fruit out of your frustrations! Your frustrations can be fruitful!

I have encouraged you in some of my other books and messages to reach out for a new life and to set new and better goals for yourself. Because ultimately, when you come to the end of your life, what you have accomplished will depend to a great degree upon what goals you have established. So if you have set goals for yourself, then I want to share with you now how you can handle frustrations as you pursue these goals, because frustration is something everyone experiences.

In the book of Romans, St. Paul wrote, *Whenever I take my journey into Spain, I will come to you"* (Romans 15:24). Well, he never got to Spain. Instead, he went to Rome and there he was made a prisoner. He died a prisoner and his dream of going to Spain never became a reality. St. Paul knew what frustration was. I am sure you know what it is. The question is, how do you handle it?

I want to offer you five simple words as an answer to that question. They rhyme, so I hope that will help you to keep them in your mind. I believe they will help you today, tomorrow, through the week, and even during the months to come.

Mrs. Schuller and I started our ministry in Garden Grove over twenty years ago. God gave us dreams and dreams are always impossible, if they come from God. When we made a commitment to an impossible dream, it was inevitable that we would experience frustration, which is a set up for God to either shape you, mold you, mature you or guide you along the way. Psalm 37:1-3 helped me enormously through my periods of personal and deep frustration:

"Fret not yourself because of the wicked . . . Trust in the Lord, and do good."

How do you face your frustrations?

1. Don't *tape* your frustrations. Many people record them, remember them and rehearse them. They tell everybody they meet how frustrated they have been and how frustrated they are. A week later they still remember their frustrations.

Recently I had a four-hour visit in my office with a man that I consider to be the greatest living psychiatrist in the world today. His name is Dr. Viktor Frankl, professor of psychiatry in Vienna, Austria. It turns out, incidentally, that Dr. and Mrs. Frankl, who make about seven trips a year to the United States, are Hour of Power fans. So I was delighted when I had a call from Dr. Frankl saying, "I'm here in America. Mrs. Frankl and I would like to visit you." And so they came.

When he drove in he saw the bulletin board and said to me, "So tomorrow you're speaking on Fruitful Frustrations. What will you tell the people?" I rattled off my points to him. "The first is, don't *tape* them; forget them, don't harbor them in your mind." He said, "That's a marvelous point, Dr. Schuller. Make sure they hear it. You might share this little story with them. When I was collaborating with Dr. Adler, the great psychiatrist who succeeded Freud, Dr. Adler liked to tell his favorite joke. There was a group of people all crowded together, sleeping on the floor of a great auditorium during the war. They were trying to sleep, but just when they were about to get to sleep, one woman would always cry out, 'Oh, God, I'm so thirsty!!' People would tell her, 'Be quiet!' But just when they were almost asleep again, she would cry out, 'Oh, God, I'm so thirsty!' Finally, one man in the darkness, said, 'Can't somebody get her a glass of water?' Rather a simple idea. In the darkness you could hear the shuffle of feet and you could hear the woman gurgle the water down. But suddenly they heard her again saying, 'Oh, God, how thirsty I was!' "

Now there is a profound psychological lesson in this little joke. Don't *tape* it. Don't hold on to it. Many people would feel emotionally lost and lonely if they didn't have past hurts and past frustrations as their morbid friends to keep them company. Don't *tape* them.

2. Don't *scrape* them. Frustrations are like mosquito bites. Now I must say in California we don't have many mosquitoes. I was born and raised in Iowa and in Iowa we had mosquitoes. Let me give you a fundamental lesson on how to handle mosquito bites: Don't scratch them. There is a distinctive, intuitive itching temptation to scratch them. But when you scratch them, you make them worse and they won't be gone in 24 hours. They'll last a week or more.

Frustrations are mosquito bites. Don't scratch them. You can make them worse.

One of my favorite stories from one of my books illustrates the point I'm trying to make: There was a very frustrated woman on a bus who spouted off and made a scene. She was rude, crude and abusive. Finally at a bus stop she got off. But just as she was getting off, the driver said, "Madame, you left something behind." She walked back up the stairs of the bus and said with a scowl on her face, "What was that? What did I leave behind?" And the bus driver said, "A very bad impression!"

3. Don't yield immediately to the *escape* temptation. Many people want to take off and run and leave the whole scene.

There have been too many wives in the 26 years I've been counselling who have said, "I wish I hadn't divorced him now." And I have had too many men say, "I wish I hadn't divorced her. The second wife was worse!"

That reminds me of a story Socrates told. Someone said to Socrates, "Should a man get married?" And Socrates replied, "By all means. Every man should have a wife. If you marry a good wife you will be thankful. And if you marry a bad wife you can become a philosopher." That's being creative, isn't it? Don't run away. Don't try to split.

A few weeks ago I was in Washington, D.C., and while I was there I stopped to visit three senators who had particularly been helped through our Hour of Power ministry. I had a very private, spiritual talk with one of these senators who was in distress. I said to him, "Senator, maybe this will help you: *Every problem has a life span. No frustration will ever enjoy eternal life. Every mountain has a top. Every hill has a crest.*" "Ah," he said, as I left, "that really helps."

In periods of frustration and in times of great difficulty, you may have the feeling that your problems will go on and on, but they won't. The question is, who is going to give in and quit first, the frustration or you? That depends upon your spirit.

The late Golda Meir said on a television interview, "All my country Israel has is spirit. We don't have petroleum dollars. We don't have mines with great wealth in the ground. We don't have the support of a world-wide public opinion that looks favorably upon us. All Israel has is the spirit of its people. And if the people lose their spirit, even the United States of America cannot save us."

Don't escape your frustrations! Hang on! Have spirit! You'll survive.

4. Don't *drape* them. You can't hide them. If you've got a feeling it's got to be, it's got to come out. The question is, how do you let it come out?

You can bury a stone, you can bury a stick and you can bury an old tin can. The can will rust, the stone will lie there and the twig will turn to dust. You can bury a stick, you can bury a stone, you can bury a can, but you cannot bury a worm. The principle is, you cannot bury and repress negative emotions and negative feelings; they will come to the surface. The problem is you're liable to blow your stack at the best people at the worst possible times.

Dr. Butler of Baylor University has said "When things get tough, don't run. People and pressures shift but the soil remains the same no matter where you go. If you can't live through this problem, you won't live through the next problem in the next place you plan to go. If you can't live through this frustration, you won't live through the next one either. People and pressures

shift but the soil remains the same no matter where you go."

Don't *tape* your frustrations. Don't *scrape* your frustrations. Don't try to *escape* your frustrations. And don't *drape* your frustrations. Don't try to hide and pretend there is nothing wrong. Develop the ability to open up before you blow up. Whatever you do, try to get to the persons who are the source of frustration in a small quiet meeting, not in public. And then open up. Try to be as kind and as Christian as you can be. And if you are unkind and unchristian in venting your frustrations, apologize. But whatever you do, don't try to harbor it. The Bible says, *"Do not let the sun go down on your anger"* (Eph. 4:26).

I don't think there are two people married that have ever had a better, healthier, happier, creative, more beautiful marriage than Mrs. Schuller and I. In our 26 years of marriage we have never let the sun go down on our frustrations with each other. We talk them out. We don't drape them or hide them. You can't! That's a prescription for failure!

5. *Shape* your frustrations and let them shape you. Every frustration has the potential to make you into something.

One of my responsibilities as pastor of my church is to be the general superintendent of the entire operation, general manager if you wish, or the captain in charge of the whole ship under Jesus Christ. From a human standpoint this means management, organization and experiencing frustrations. And not inevitably and not infrequently it means frustrations with people on how to handle them. I made a decision a long time ago I would never fire anyone and I have the power to do so. I said, "Lord, you do the firing and the hiring. And if I have a frustration I will assume, Lord, that it means that I have to learn something from this or I have to grow from it or I have to be taught humility or patience. You take it away if it has to be."

I like the story of the man who saw a 100-year-old grandfather clock with a huge weight at the bottom. He watched that old clock having to push that weight back and forth and thought, "That's a terrible burden for such an old clock. It moves so slow." Obviously it was tiring to the old antique. So he opened the glass cage and lifted the huge weight off to relieve the old clock. But the clock said, "Why did you take my weight off?" And the old man replied, "Well, I know it was a burden to you." But the old clock exclaimed, "Oh no! My weight is what keeps me going!"

The writer of Hebrews wrote, *"Those whom (the Lord) loves, he reproves and chastens"* (see Hebrews 12:6). Because God really loves you, you will experience frustrations. God has to frequently frustrate us either to teach us humility or to restrain us. *Your weights are what keep you going!*

Let your frustrations shape you. Ask God, "Lord, what must I learn from this?" And I can tell you if nothing more, you will have to learn patience.

A couple of weeks ago I made a call on a young lady who became a Christian through our Hour of Prayer telecast and now she is dying. She said to me, "Dr. Schuller, I don't know why I've lasted as long as I have. But I really believe there is a purpose for it. I was frightened when I first heard that I had cancer and I wasn't going to live more than ten months. I was so afraid that I would be a burden emotionally on my relatives and friends. Then I heard you talk about possibilities in all adversities and I dared to believe that I could be an inspiration to my people until my dying day. So every time someone comes to my side I make it a point to say 'Lord, how can I minister to my relatives and friends who care for me now hour after hour?' " And she is doing a beautiful job. She is no burden on her loved ones. She is no burden on her family. *She is the weight that keeps them going!* Her soul has been shaped into a gorgeous thing of beauty and she is an inspiration to everyone who has the privilege of taking care of her.

*Shape* your frustrations and let them shape you. This takes a lot of faith. And that's what some of you probably need. Some of you probably do not have a relationship with God.

Dr. Frankl told me, "Dr. Schuller, there are unconditional possibilities for meaning in life to the last breath. You only have a relationship with Almighty God and know that you are in His will. He is shaping your life. You belong to Him. You have been saved by our Lord Himself. You are God's child. Then His Holy Spirit fills you, directs you and leads you."

I asked him, "Dr. Frankl, how can I make people believe in God Today?" And he said, "I'll tell you what is helpful to me and it might be helpful to your people. Many people cannot feel God's presence until I tell them this: Man is like an actor on a stage. You are born and you are on stage until the end. But it is a stage. The spotlight is bright and it is on you. The houselights are dark. You come onto the stage and you do not see the audience. They have no lines to speak. You do not hear them or see them. There is only a black hole. But you are very much aware of a presence judging you.

"That black hole is also encouraging you and probably inspiring you and that knowledge energizes you and motivates you and guides you because it determines your behavior while you are on the stage. And if you keep your mind on pleasing the unseen in the black hole, before you know it, the end comes. And there is an applause. And the lights go on and you see the faces.

"So it is with you and me. God is there in effect like a black hole. You cannot see His face. You cannot hear His voice. But you know there is a presence watching you who cares about your performance and who is silently judging you. It restrains you. It inspires you. It motivates you. It encourages you."

Oh yes, there is a God in that black hole. Let me give you a clue: Put the light on for a minute and you know what you will see? You will see a Man on a cross. You will see Jesus Christ reaching out to you.

# Discover How You Can Turn Activity Into Energy

# 1

## *Recycle Your Energy*

The Bible is filled with many statements indicating that our relationship to God vitally affects our human energy output. The prophet Isaiah wrote:

"They that wait upon the Lord shall renew their strength. They shall mount up with wings as eagles; they shall run and not be weary; and they shall walk and not faint" (Isaiah 40:31)

St. Paul wrote to the people in Ephesus that he was praying for them,

"That out of his glorious, unlimited resources He will give you the mighty inner strengthening of his Holy Spirit" (Ephesians 3:16)

Emerson wrote, "The world belongs to the energetic." And Sir Thomas Buxton agreed when he said, "The longer I live, the more deeply I am convinced that what makes the difference between one man and another, the great and the insignificant, is energy; that invincible determination, a purpose that once formed, nothing can take away. This energetic quality will do anything that is meant by God to be done in this world, and no talent, no training, no opportunity, no circumstance will make any man a man without it."

Obviously, there is a difference in energy levels from one person to another. The question is "Why?" What makes the difference? Can anyone learn to live on a more dynamic energetic level?

I want to share with you some principles on how to

recycle your energy so that you'll never really suffer from real fatigue again. The honest truth is that hard work does not produce fatigue, and real rest does not heal fatigue. Psychological observations and studies show that nine tenths of all fatigue among sedentary people is psychological and emotional. And that means it is also theological, because you cannot divide psychology from theology. You cannot take the human soul and slice it into sections and say, "This section is the brain, this section is the emotion, this section is the soul, and this section is the mind that needs to be healed by psychiatry." The true person is a whole human being, and sectionalism is improper when we think of healing humans. If it is a psychological problem then it is a theological problem.

I am blessed by God with tremendous energy and have been all my life. But I don't think that I genetically have more energy than other people. My testimony to you is this very simple thing: *"In Him* (meaning in God and in Christ) *we live* (that means we are really alive), *and move* (instead of sitting down and slouching and sleeping lazily), *and have our being"* (Acts 17:28). The truth is, God is the cosmic source of all spiritual energy. And when we are close to God and in tune with Him, we tap the source of energy.

What I must say at the outset of this message is quite simple: Some people are tired because they're afraid they're going to get tired. And because they're afraid they're going to get tired, they don't spend their energy because they want to save it. And because they're not spending it and because they're saving it, they're constantly fatigued. If you don't have energy, the best way to get it is to give it out.

When I woke up this morning, it was still black outdoors. I had no idea what time it was. Then I heard our clock and I knew it was 5:00 a.m. "Boy, I'm still tired," I thought. "I'm still tired, and I know I won't go back to sleep now." (What a negative thought! If you think you won't go back to sleep, naturally you won't go back to sleep!) So I had a battle with myself on the pillow. And then I thought, "If I want energy, the best way to get it is not to spend another sixty minutes in bed. The best way to get it is to jump out of bed, get my running suit on and take a long run."

Actually, I was too tired to run, which was only proof of the fact that that was exactly what I had to do. So I jumped out of bed, got my running suit on and started running off into the hills. Everything went fine until in the utter darkness I turned down the wrong road, and for the first time, I got lost while running.

But I kept running and when I reached a deadend, I turned around. It was starting to get light and soon I recognized some landmarks. Before long, I found myself at my front gate—exactly 65 minutes after I started my uninterrupted run. When I got in the house and into my hot shower, the blood was in every corner of my skin. I was more energetic than ever! I got energy by giving out energy! Energy is right there inside of you! All you have to do is prime the pump.

Let me give it to you in one sentence:

## WHAT YOU GET IS WHAT YOU GIVE!

You can turn it around and it still holds true:

## WHAT YOU GIVE IS WHAT YOU WILL GET!

Now that is a universal principle. If you want love from people, you have to give love. And the love that

you get in return from other people is going to be in proportion to what you give.

If you have financial problems, give money away to somebody who is doing something beautiful for God. Money given is like a seed planted—it will come back to you with an increase. *"And the measure you give will be the measure you get"* (Matthew 7:2).

It's true for love. It's true for your money. It's true with your job. And it's true for human energy. What you give is what you will get! I call it recycled energy.

# 2

## Energy Is A
## Matter Of Attitude

Several years ago, I was in Miami, Florida, to deliver a lecture at a large convention. Earlier on the program was a major address by one of the most powerful senators in the United States. Everyone would recognize his name, for it is almost a household word. I arrived early to hear his speech, and then went up to him to thank him, for it was a great speech.

I was so impressed with the man's tremendous energy. He was in his early 60's at that time, and not too long before he had discovered he had cancer. But he bounded up that stage with energy, and he spoke for 55 minutes with energy.

As I thanked him for his talk, he took hold of my arm and with misty eyes said, "You'll never know what Hour of Power ministry has done for me and for the rest of us in Washington, D.C." And that touched me very humbly and beautifully.

As we talked, I was impressed with the fact that energy is not a matter of age—it is a matter of attitude!

It's not a matter of general health, because I see people who have had major surgery and are battling cancer, and they have loads of energy. What is the key? It's attitude! And the secret to an energetic attitude is in the reality of this verse:

*"In Him we live, and move, and have our being"* (Acts 17:28).

Do you need energy? Give it out and you'll get it back. Put out energy and you'll end up with more energy than you gave out. It's really true!

Now if it's true on an organic level, it is also true on the spiritual level. If you need more energy it probably means you need more faith in God. Because if you have a closer relationship with God, you'll be dreaming great dreams and attempting great things. Anybody who loves and moves in the will of God is going to be a high-energy person. *"For it is God who is at work within you, giving you the will and the power to achieve His purpose"* (See Philippians 2:13).

If you aren't energetic enough on the job, for instance, probably you're not giving your job enough. You're probably checking in as late as you can, checking out as quickly as you can and doing as little on the job as you can possibly get by with. Well, obviously in that kind of a situation you're not going to be enthused. *And enthusiasm is energy!* The word *enthusiasm is* made up of *en-theos*—in God.

Is Friday the best day of your week? Do you start getting a little energy on Friday evening, more energy on Saturday and a lot of kick and get up and go on Saturday night? And on Sunday you've got quite a bit of it left, but on Monday morning when you have to go back to work, do you feel tired again?

*"In Him we live, and move, and have our being."* What it means is that you have to bring Christ into your life and apply Christ in your job so that you turn your job into a ministry.

Do you need energy? Do you want to recycle it? Give

it out! It'll come back! Begin by making sure that you are in a close relationship with God and yourself.

Is there some secret sin in your life? If so, there will be guilt, and this guilt will block the flow of real power and energy.

Real power comes electrically through positive and negative wires. Let me say, the same is true spiritually. If you want dynamic energy, you have to be in the will of God. If you want to be in the will of God, you have to have the positive and the negative wires together. That means you have to have the power to say "no" to something that is wrong.

Recently I was asked to attend a board meeting at another corporation of which I am not a member of the board. The meeting was with a couple of high-powered realtors, a landowner and the landowner's lawyer. I wasn't in the meeting three minutes when the lawyer be-

came very upset about something. I was shocked. I could tell that in that kind of a mental climate there were such negative vibrations that if I stayed around I'd be fatigued in ten minutes, and I didn't want to waste my energy. I think I said something to this effect: "When you are able to address yourselves in positive terms and with enthusiasm in a calm and reflective mind, I will be happy to return and rejoin the assembly." And with that I made a hasty exit. I could feel fatigue hanging in the room because of the negative vibrations from the cantankerous, negative-thinking lawyer.

I came back into the room a minute later to find the lawyer storming out. (Miracles do happen!) But as soon as he got out, the quibbling and the quarrelling started again. So I suggested something which I hoped would be positive bait—and it was. They all got talking about the project that brought them together. And as they started talking about the project, they started dreaming. And as they dreamed, they got excited. And as they got excited, they got more enthusiastic. And when they started putting their ideas out, energy came back, and it was just fantastic to see the transformation that took place in that room!

Do you want energy? Power comes through the positive and the negative wires. The negative is to pull away from anything that would produce anxiety, fears, anger or guilt. The positive is drawn to anything that would produce the power to dream dreams and to get involved in projects and get excited.

There are people who use an enormous amount of energy to resist God's Holy Spirit when He tries to move into their lives. And what happens? *God stays out and they stay tired.* It's that simple.

Let me sum up, so far, with this sentence:

GREAT ACTIVITY IS NOT CAUSED
BY GREAT ENERGY,
BUT GREAT ACTIVITY PRODUCES
GREAT ENERGY.

What you give is what you get, and what you get is what you'll give. If you want the energy of God in your life, give your life to God and give your life to Jesus Christ. He'll come in and you'll be in tune with an infinite cosmic source of unending, unlimited energy that will recycle itself as you do His happy work.

# 3

## *More Energy For Better Living*

There is no doubt about it—your relationship with God is a vital factor in your own human energy level.

Sometime ago a friend of ours, Don Sutton, the ace Los Angeles Dodger pitcher, was here and told us how every professional athlete looks for the edge. "Because," he said, "to really be a great success all you have to do is be just a little better than everybody else. It's that simple. All you need is the edge on the competition." "And," he said, "Jesus Christ gives me the winner's edge!" And He does, because God produces that dynamic flow of energy.

St. Paul I think was teaching this when he said, *"I can do all things through Christ who strengthens me"* (see Philippians 4:13). *"In God we live and move and have our being"* (Acts 17:28). *"The Lord is my strength and my song, and He has become my salvation"* (Exodus 15:2).

Physical energy, of course, is a matter of keeping your body in good tone, good tune, exercising right and eating right. But it requires not only physical exercise, it must also have spiritual exercise. Because if a person is healthy he's a whole person. So your relationship with God definitely affects your energy level. It gives you that extra edge.

I can explain how it works. If you have a relationship with God, you're constantly excited. Excitement is a dynamic, natural energy. You say to me, "Yes, Dr. Schuller, but what about the problems?" And that's what's so exciting!

Possibility thinking is not a pollyanna philosophy that ignores the reality of problems. Possibility thinking says that every problem is pregnant with possibilities. Problems turn me on! I don't think anything would be more dull or boring than if I had no problems!

I said to a group of friends recently at a banquet in a local hotel, "I'm so excited because today I am facing the biggest problem I've ever faced in my ministry. And that really turns me on!" The problem we have in our ministry is that our sanctuary is so small that we have people standing in the aisles and in the back. And it happens every Sunday. We have what we call a growth-restricting problem. But do you know what? This problem makes me excited, *because every problem is an opportunity*. It's an opportunity for us to think bigger and reach higher. I don't believe we would ever grow unless God pushed us into it.

Robert Ardray put it this way, "Every human being has three deep needs—the need for identity, the need for security and the need for stimulation." Now these three deep inner needs oftentimes conflict with each other. If I were to submit a test to you and say, "What is your deepest need—stimulation, security or identity?" Most people would opt for security. In other words, they want to be sure they are secure, physically and emotionally, in their interpersonal relations, in their jobs and in their finances. Security is the number one thing they're after.

But here's the problem: The road that's marked "Security" is a cul-de-sac that ends with one big sign that says, "Boredom." If you achieve ultimate security, you will achieve ultimate boredom. The only way to escape from boredom is to expose yourself to the stimulation of some risk, some adventure or some mountain.

I've discovered in my life that possibility thinking turns me on with energy. Why? Because it helps me to escape from the road of security and commits me to the road of stimulation!

Let me illustrate very graphically about the biggest problem I have ever faced in my life. When my wife and I came to start our church twenty years ago, we had a dream of a church of 6,000 members. We thought it would take that many people to support the program, and to minister to the needs of all the people here who are hurting. It would take that many people to teach the Sunday School, to call on the sick in the hospital and to run a 24-hour telephone counselling service. And we thought that it would probably take us forty years to build up a church of 6,000 members, and so we had a plan. We planned to win 150 members a year, and in forty years, by the time I was 68, we would have 6,000 members. Then we would probably retire, leaving behind a great work that would continue to be a throbbing heart of love in the heart of this county. We thought that would make our life worthwhile.

So that was our dream. I did not, at that time, know the Alfred North Whitehead principle, which says: "Great dreams of great dreamers are never fulfilled, they are always transcended." I didn't know at that time that great dreams of great dreamers are God's dreams. And I didn't realize that God is always dreaming much bigger than I am. Because I want to play it safe, I want the stimulation, but I want to be secure, too. So I don't allow myself to dream so big that it really becomes reckless. I keep my dreams smaller, now knowing that God's dreams are always bigger. And what's happened after twenty years? We have succeeded! And what is success? When you succeed, you don't eliminate problems, you inherit bigger ones!

We had a master plan when we came to this church. We called for a sanctuary to seat nearly 2,000 people and that would handle 6,000 members running multiple services. A year ago we could see the growth curve and we made growth projections. But I turned my back on it because the only solution to that problem was to build a bigger auditorium, and I frankly didn't want to build any more buildings. I'm 48 years old, and it seems like I've been building buildings for twenty years. Not only that, but I happen to love this sanctuary. I worked on it with Richard Neutra, who is now deceased, and our sanctuary and tower are the world's finest walk-in,

drive-in church. Someday it will be a historical monument. And Richard Neutra said this was the finest thing he had ever done.

Did you know that this church is the only church that is photographed in the Soviet Union? In their book of great architecture of our century, they had to include a church. It is internationally great. So I can't get interested in building buildings unless they are excellent.

I was taught a principle at Hope College, and that is, "Don't do something great; too many people already are. Only do something that excels." Excellence produces excitement. Excitement produces energy. Energy creates momentum. And momentum makes things happen!

A year ago I could see we needed a new building, and I didn't want to think about it because of the costs. I knew we didn't have the money. I was a classical negative thinker.

Well, I finally tackled the problem. The church board has unanimously agreed that we're going to solve this problem somehow. We are consulting at the present time with three of the greatest architects alive in the world today. All three are interested in the prospect of designing this new auditorium, which will be on the lawn north of our tower. It will be so beautiful that it will be an experience for people to worship there 100 years from now. It will make it possible for us to reach unchurched people in our territory and in our community.

Every morning since the first of January, 1975, I have been in the pulpit, and I can tell you, there hasn't been a Sunday when I haven't seen people turn and leave because it got too cold for them outdoors, or they were too tired to stand up in the aisle. I'm only 48, and I'm expecting to be here at least twenty more years. So finally we've decided we're going to build the building. All we need, we conclude, is $5 million. And we only have a couple hundred thousand dollars right now.

But that isn't the big problem. If I had cancer of the brain, then that would be a problem. But I'd like to make an announcement: We are going to be receiving a gift of $1 million! Isn't that great? Now I must hasten to say at this point, I don't know who is going to give it yet. But it's coming! I can feel it! Because I feel the problem so heavily. *And every time you've got a big problem, you're on the edge of a miracle!*

Nineteen years ago I stood on the sticky tar paper roof of the snack bar of the Orange Drive-In Theatre, and I said, "We are going to build a Tower of Hope. It will cost about $1 million or more, and it's coming. I don't know where it's coming from, but it's coming. And when we get it, it's going to be filled with people praying for people every minute of every hour of every day and night. We don't have any money, but God isn't poor. And He waits to pour out His abundance, but He doesn't give His riches to small-thinking people. He only gives it to those who believe big, and Lord, am I believing big!"

# 4

## The Bigger The Problem,
## The Bigger The Miracle!

Great things are going to happen in your life as you tap into God's resource of energy! Great miracles are going to happen. I can't tell you how, but I can affirm to you with confidence that it is going to happen!

When you think this way you become energized because, you see, some people are fatigued because they don't dream any dreams. They don't dream any dreams because they want to play it safe. They don't want to get involved. They don't want to take chances. They don't want to run the risk of failure. They'd be so terribly embarrassed if later on they had to admit they were wrong. And so rather than think big and talk big, they play it safe and boy, are they dull! You will never find possibility thinkers boring, I'll tell you that! Some people are dead, lacking energy, because they don't dream great dreams.

Then there are those that draw close enough to God until God reveals His dreams, but then they don't dare to make the decision to do anything about it. And procrastination produces fatigue. Indecision is the most tiring thing you could experience emotionally.

The bigger the problem, the bigger the miracle. And I don't know how God is going to use me in it, but when you're standing on the edge of something great, how can you have more energy for better living? First, find a problem of your own or a problem that somebody else has. Look for a problem that seems to be unsolvable. If you can, try to find a problem that from a

human standpoint would take a miracle to get it out of the way. Then begin to pray, "Oh God, I want to thank you for this problem. Great good can come out of it. Oh God, I want to thank you for what's impossible with men is possible with you. I want to thank you for the miracles you are preparing. Oh God, I want to thank you for the faith you're giving to me now."

Pray, seek God's guidance and what's going to happen? You'll get a dream to pursue. I have a dream to build this great new church, so that our ministry can go on and on and grow for the next twenty years. Find a dream. Once you've got that dream and you know it's God's dream for your life, then be daring. Dare to say it. Let the redeemed of the Lord say so. Announce to the whole world that it's going to happen. That is faith in action! And it'll prove to people that you're not afraid of being embarrassed by failure as much as you are of being afraid of thinking too small, not having enough faith, to do something great for God.

Dream, then have nerve and be daring. And then make the decision. Let me tell you, fatigue is produced

in many lives because they have no dreams; they're not excited about anything. They're not excited about anything because they cautiously try to avoid their problems and the problems of other people, because they don't want to get involved, and they don't want to make the sacrifices, and they don't want to be unselfish, and they don't want to give. So they play it safe, they ride the security road and they land up with a meaningless life. And when they die, who cares? "Only one life will soon be passed. Only what's done for Christ will last."

Some people are fatigued because they don't have any dreams, and they don't have any dreams because they avoid problems. And others have dreams, but they don't make a decision to give it all they've got. Indecision is the great fatigue producer. Make the decision to give it all you've got, and you will be astounded at the energy that will come out of you.

William James said, "You have enormous untapped powers that you probably will never tap, because most people never run far enough on their first wind to ever find out they've got a second."

I've discovered the secret to tapping enormous resources of energy in my relationship with Jesus Christ. I believe that He strengthens me, in the inner mind, through the Holy Spirit. St. Paul said, *"I can do all things through Christ who strengthens me"* (see Philippians 4:13). Literally, physically, He does!

Become an authentic Christian today. Invite Jesus Christ to be your Savior, your God and your friend. And wow! What power and energy you will discover for your life!

# Discover
## How To Get Your
## Priorities Straight

# 1

## *How To Succeed Where You Have Always Failed Before*

Abraham Lincoln told the story of a blacksmith who took a piece of red hot iron and hammered it on an anvil, not knowing exactly what he would make out of it. He first thought he would make a sword, but it didn't turn out very well. Then he tried to bend it and make a horseshoe, but that didn't work out either. So he just hammered and hammered until finally the piece of iron was good for nothing. He had hammered the life out of it and still had nothing to show for his effort. It was one big waste. So he took it in the tongs, for it was still hot, and stuck it in a pail of water. As he did, he said, "At least I can make a fizzle out of it!"

Perhaps that is how you feel sometimes. I get thousands of letters each week and I know that a lot of people feel that way about themselves. They have just made a fizzle out of life. They have no priorities, no goals, no sense of direction—life is nothing but a fizzle!

If you feel that way, I have good news for you. If you have been making a fizzle out of your life, you can now start to make a success out of it! You can overcome that basic blockage that holds you back at each failure point!

St. Paul wrote,

"Do not be conformed to this world, but be transformed by the renewal of your mind." (Romans 12:2)

What does he mean? For one thing, if you have tried and failed and tried and failed, chances are you are trying within your own strength and power alone, and that is what St. Paul means by "conforming to the world." In the Bible, the "world" is a word that basically means the total aggregate collection of corporate human beings who are unrelated to God; and who are, therefore, basically skeptical, negative-thinking, cynical people. They are the mass of people who have no dynamic, healthy, vital relationship with God. As a result, they become cynical people, who distrust themselves, others and God.

Some of these people are that way because they never developed trust in the first phase of their life—they did not have a loving mother during their first year of life. If this frightens some of you because you, perhaps, did not have a loving mother during that period of your life, and you happen to know enough about your family history to know that that was the case, *there is hope for you!* You can be healed. You can be helped if you are highly motivated, even if you suffered emotional damage in the first or second phase of life. If you didn't learn self-confidence or decision making in the second phase of your life, there is still hope for you. Your life can be transformed. There's no doubt about it!

The Bible says, do not be conformed to "worldly" thinking. This is the kind of mentality that says, "I can't do it. I guess I was born this way. I'll always have this character defect. There is nothing that can be done about it." *"Do not be conformed to this world but be transformed by the renewal of your mind!"* Now that's the key to starting to succeed where you have always failed before.

I have listed seven different points in life that might be areas where you are failing or a reason for your failing. In other words, if you want to start succeeding and stop failing in whatever your goals or priorities might be, check these seven points. I have picked words that rhyme, hoping that you might remember them.

Some people keep failing when they could be succeeding because of *blights, frights, fights, nights, lights, sights or flights.* I want to hinge my thoughts on these rhyming words and I think you will understand how you can renew your mind and be transformed accordingly.

## 1. Blights.

If you have failed and then tried and failed again, it is probably because of the *blights*. Almost everyone recognizes his imperfections. Many people develop this sense of imperfectionism which leads to an inferiority complex and a lack of self-confidence when they are very little children. Chances are in your childhood, when you were two, three and four years old, you had the idea that mother, God, Jesus and daddy were perfect. Somehow you had that confused image; you probably never escaped it. They were perfect and you therefore know that you are not as good a person as your father or mother. And comparing yourself against the infantile impression in this unrealistic image you hold of them probably gives you this sense of inferiority. With this sense of inferiority, what you really are saying is, "I don't deserve to succeed. I'm not good enough." And this can be the beginning of a *will to fail*. Even though you say you want to succeed, at the deepest level, you probably do not want to succeed because you really don't think you deserve it.

I had an interesting counselling session just before Christmas. I was called to visit a home because the father and mother watch the Hour of Power and it is their only church. The man has had a fabulous life here in Southern California. He is a very famous person and is, in material terms, a super successful man. He is now in poor health, 82 years of age, and it looks like he is coming to the end of his life. With misty eyes he said to me, "The sadness in my life, Dr. Schuller, is that I never was the man my father was."

He told me the story of his Scottish father. "My father was a good man. He could pray in church and at home and he would always take us all to church. Every morning we would have thirty minutes of prayer and Bible reading around the family table. My father was only a farmer, but what a great man he was! How he could pray in public! And interspersed in his prayers were the most beautiful Bible verses. I never, never came close to that.

"I came to America as a young man. I had no money and I needed a job. I had to work hard. And then to make more money, I hired people. Then to help these people I hired more people and the business expanded. Before I realized it the business got bigger and bigger. I couldn't cut it down because there were a lot of people depending on my business for their livelihood. Suddenly, here I am, 82 years old, and I couldn't offer a prayer out loud for anything." The man was very sad.

I looked at him and said, "John, I have a revelation for you. I think it came from God. I think He wants me to tell you something. What you said about your father is beautiful. Now let's look at your life. One of the things you did among your grand, vast enterprises was build houses. Tens of thousands of people today are living in beautiful houses in Southern California because you made them. You gave hundreds of thousands of people paychecks and they were able to go home and buy food and clothing for their children. There are tens of thousands of Christmas trees today at hearthsides in the homes you built. Think of all the people, the homes and the families that have shelter and food and clothing and a little savings account because of your life's work. John, here's the revelation: *Your father was good at offering prayers, but you've been great in answering them!* In the sight of God, who is the greatest, you or your dad?" "Oh, that helps, that really helps," he sighed.

Most of us have some *blights*. We think we don't deserve to succeed. *Blights* may hold us back. Affirm that you are great and by God's grace through Jesus Christ you can be.

## 2. Frights.

This is the fear of failure or the fear of competition.

Dr. Robert Steinberg, a noted psychiatrist in Southern California, discussed a particular case with me recently. A child in the third stage of life is attached to the mother and feels that he competes with the father. There can evolve, at this stage, the fear of success. If the child is told to do something, he is afraid that if he succeeds he may be competing with his father. I said to Dr. Steinberg, "Really, Bob, do you think a child, four years old, thinks that logically and that such profound concepts can go through such an infant's mind?" Bob really straightened me out. "Why, Dr. Schuller, you know better than that. A four year old is not an infant!"

Dr. Berkowitz tells a marvelous story in his book, *How to Be Awake and Alive*. A young man he called Chuck had all kinds of promise to be a successful man in the field of acting. Every time he got a great offer to play a part and they got down to signing the contract, the man would become very upset about the way the producer handled the negotiations, or the way the agent handled it, and he would blow up about a little detail and the whole opportunity would fizzle out. Finally, Dr. Berkowitz told him, "Imagine that you're in your hometown. There is the theatre, there is the marquee, there is your name in lights and you are performing on stage. Imagine your father and mother walking across the street. They see your name in lights." At that point this young man jumped out of his chair, red-faced with anger and hatred. "No! No!" he shouted. "They don't deserve it! They don't deserve to see me as a success!" And he tripped it. He let the cat out of the bag. On a subliminal level he hated his father and mother. He wanted to fail in order to punish them.

### 3. Fights.

There is an English movie called, "The Loneliness of the Long Distance Runner." It portrays a young man in school. Motivated by his headmaster, whom he thought was also a friend, the youth runs his heart out in track. He gradually does even better and it begins to look as though he is going to be one of the greatest runners in England.

Shortly before one of his most crucial races, the headmaster, who was his coach and supposedly a friend, betrayed him. When it came time for the big race, this young man ran off ahead of everybody else. As he came close to the wire where he was destined to win, he suddenly stopped in his tracks, put his arms across his chest and just stood there while the other runners ran around him to win. He deliberately chose to fail.

In the movie he looks at the headmaster and glares with rage as he says, "I got even with you!"

It's amazing how many people want to fail. That is their way of getting even and fighting back. Yet, in reality, they are the losers. Is this your problem?

### 4. Nights.

Maybe it's the dark times in your past—the times when you were hurt or disillusioned—that are holding you back. Maybe that's what makes you fail constantly.

I wrote these words in one of my books: "How do you handle your past failures? Suppose you tried again and again but failed. What does that mean? Failure doesn't mean you'll never make it. It does mean you have to do it differently. Failure doesn't mean you don't have it. It does mean you have to make some deep changes. Failure doesn't mean you'll never succeed. It does mean it will take longer. Failure doesn't mean

you're a fool to try again. It does mean you have the courage to keep making noble commitments and great resolutions. Failure doesn't mean God doesn't answer prayers. It does mean that God has a better idea."

Check your *blights*, *frights*, *fights* and your *nights*.

Other people are held back by their *lights*.

## 5. Lights.

They've had a little success and they're satisfied. They wanted to prove something to themselves. They've done it and then quit. I know people that have reached a certain level and stopped there. They're bedazzled by their own success. They think they are so successful when actually they've only reached the first rung of the ladder of their invisible ultimate potential. If the nights and the dark experiences hold some people back, the lights and the little successes hold others back.

Dr. Viktor Frankl, the great psychiatrist from Vienna, Austria, has said, "The *is* must never catch up with the *ought*."

## 6. Sights.

This also holds some people back. They think too short; they think too small. Almost always the solution to the problem is to think longer or to think bigger or to think deeper. Their sights are too small.

May I repeat my favorite story? I can't think of anything that illustrates my point better than the story of the man fishing on the pier. A tourist came and watched him. When he caught a fish, he would get out a measuring tape and measure it. The little ones he would throw in his bucket. If they were over ten inches, he threw them back in the water.

The tourist couldn't stand it. "What's the big idea?" He asked. "You keep the little ones and you throw the big ones away! What's the meaning of it all?" The fisherman looked at him and said, "Well, my frying pan is only ten inches long!"

Think bigger. Almost always that's where you'll find the solution to your problems.

## 7. Flights.

What do I mean by that? *I mean not being willing to make the commitment deeply.*

Dr. Norman Vincent Peale says in one of his marvelous books, "Almost always, people fail not because they lack the possibility of inner strength, but they fail because they just don't give it all they've got. They hold back a little bit." You can succeed when you've always been failing if you'll just get that inner strength. Stop flying; settle down. Begin by avoiding these *flights*. Make the commitment.

How do you stand with God? How do you stand with Jesus Christ? What's holding you back? Maybe it's the fact that just when you are ready to make the ultimate decision that could solve your problem once and for all, you back off. I know that ultimately you will never be the person you want to be, you will never solve the problems that you've never solved before, until you make a real deep commitment to God and to Jesus Christ. And that's how your total life can be renewed and your mind and your life transformed. But some people are flighty. Just as soon as they get ready to be challenged to make a big, costly, daring commitment, they take off.

You listen to me when I talk about psychology and psychiatry and when I tell my funny little stories. But when I start zeroing in to say, "My friend, have you ever received Jesus Christ into your life? Have you ever turned your life over to Jesus Christ and to God Almighty?" that's when you want to turn me off. You get flighty like a bird. Well, I dare you right now not to turn me off. Because you may be turning off the magic key. When your commitments are right, you're ready to work on your priorities.

# 2

## Guidelines For Getting Your Priorities Straight

*There is a better life for you* and I want you to know that it can happen if you will discover the principles for successfully arranging your priorities. Because ultimately *where you are* and *where you will go* depends upon what goals you have set or will set for yourself, and what priorities you have. To get your priorities straight, we must work with some principles of goal setting.

The secret of success is to set the right goals and priorities and never take your eye off of them. As Jesus said, *"No man, having put his hand to the plough, and looking back, is fit for the kingdom of God"* (Luke 9:62). Set a goal and keep your eye on it.

The words I share with you first are from the book of Deuteronomy:

"I have set before you life or death, blessing or curse. Oh, that you would choose life" (Deut. 30:19).

You can choose to live or you can choose to die. You can choose to be a blessing or you can choose to be the kind of a person that is a curse to those who have to live with you. *"I have set before you life or death, blessing or curse. Oh, that you would choose life."*

The exciting thing about this is that everyone is given the power and the freedom, by God, to choose what kind of a life he wants to live, what he wants to accomplish and what he wants to achieve. It all begins with setting your priorities in order and identifying your goals.

Four times each year we conduct Institutes for Successful Church Leadership. Over 5,000 ministers and church leaders from around the world have attended these institutes and a thousand more will attend this year alone.

I received a letter recently from a pastor in Australia. He wrote: "Never before, until I attended the Institute, had I heard of possibility thinking. These concepts have radically changed my ministry. You see, the Bishop told me that his prognosis for my church was gradual decline and closure, with the remnant of the congregation being split between two neighboring churches until they became small enough to close them also. And the process would be repeated. I was so determined I could not be a part of such a death process. One alternative was to quit; the other alternative was to go to this institute in America as the last desperate possibility."

Upon his return to Australia, the first thing he decided to do was set a goal for increasing the Christmas congregation. And in fact, his attendance was twenty-five percent more than last year. He tells how they changed their whole concept of worship and how they changed their whole format. The church is starting to grow and it's going to have a great success.

The mental attitude you have will determine the goals you set. And the goals you set more than anything else will determine your priorities and where you will land up in life. This is true, whether it's a spiritual goal, a personal goal, a professional goal or a family goal. It makes no difference.

Sigmund Freud said that goals are very dangerous, because if you set goals and then don't make them, you'll experience failure. This will annihilate your self-respect and you will become a very sick and neurotic person. Freud was basically anti-goal. But Dr. Viktor Frankl, from Vienna, Austria, says that goals are great. Indeed, it can be quite disastrous if you set a goal and don't make it and have a negative attitude toward it. But not *reaching your goal isn't as dangerous as not having a goal*.

He likes to point to the Old Testament story of how God always kept a pillar of fire in front of the people at night and a cloud by day to pull the people forward. That's what goals do to us. You never catch up with the

cloud. You never catch up with the fire. And the *is* must never catch up with the *ought*. If you set a goal and then reach it and can't expand it, you start dying.

I want to give you seven principles for successful goal setting.

1. *Begin with possibility thinking.*

When you set your private goals, your personal goals, your spiritual goals or your professional goals, begin with possibility thinking. And what is that? Possibility thinking is the assumption that if it is a beautiful idea, if it is a great thing for God, if it would help people who are suffering, then of course, there must be a way! So goals always rise out of problems—never out of "ego-tripping!" Matthew 19:26 says, *"With men this is impossible, but with God all things are possible."* In setting your goals assume that it is possible, even though it may appear impossible.

Adela Rogers St. John has written a marvelous book entitled, *Some Are Born Great.* In it she tells the story of Rachael Carson, who wrote, *Silent Spring.* In the book there is this dialogue between Alice and the Red Queen. Alice says, "One can't believe impossible things." And the queen says, "I dare say, you haven't had much practice. When I was your age, I always did it for half an hour a day. Why, sometimes I believed in as many as six impossible things before I had breakfast." "And that," says Rachael Carson, "is a very necessary thing to do and to know. If you start believing in impossible things before breakfast, the first thing you know by dinner time they are not impossible anymore." It begins with possibility thinking.

2. *Let your value system guide you.*

Your goals must be *compatible* or they will be *combatible.* Unless they are compatible with your own deepest value system, they will be combatible. Then you will have tension, guilt and anxiety inside of you and you won't be able to succeed. At your deepest level you must ask yourself, what did I believe as a child? What did I believe as a little boy? What did I believe as a little girl? What were the deepest, purest, greatest ideals

I ever looked up to? Perhaps today you're cynical or tarnished. Maybe you've separated yourself from these great moral ideals that you once held. I say to you, in setting your goals, go back to your highest values and your highest ideals and make certain that whatever goals you are setting for yourself professionally, spiritually or in any way, they are compatible with these high, God-inspired ideals. If they are not, you won't be able to give it all you've got!

That's why ultimately only the honest man enjoys happy success. Compatible or combatible—make sure your goals harmonize with your value system. Then you will come to the end of your life with pride behind you, love around you and hope ahead of you.

Recently I took a trip down to Mexico to go marlin fishing. I was the guest of some very dear friends; Rev. Bob Pierce, one of the great spiritual giants of the 20th century; and his friend and mine, Chuck Walters who has been influenced by my books, and runs a resort near the cape of Baja, California.

I must say before I reveal the results of my adventure that you must see it in its proper perspective. First of all, for some reason the marlin hadn't been hitting for a couple of days. And you must bear in mind that I had never hooked a marlin anyway so I would require a great deal of experience if such had been the case. Furthermore, when we were out on the second day there were four of us fishing on the stern. Three of those in the group were professionals—they were all experts at king-size fish catching. I was the only beginner. And when I tell you that none of those fellows caught a marlin or a sailfish, then I think you have the right perspective. But I must also tell you that I practiced possibility thinking, which I'm not sure they did.

We had our four lines out of the stern with the live mackerels bouncing at the end. I was on one corner, Chuck Walters was on another corner, and Bob Pierce and our other friend were still further away. Suddenly, Chuck said, "Look at the fin! Here comes one!" It was a massive marlin, heading straight for the first bait, belonging to Chuck Walters. The marlin came close but for some reason skipped Chuck's line and headed for the second one. For some reason he also skipped the second bait and went right for the third one belonging to Dr. Bob Pierce. Knowing what a great Christian Bob Pierce is, I knew the marlin would go for his line! But he didn't take it either, and that left only mine—bang! He hit it. And I had a hook-up! I must say, with all due modesty, I landed him, all 150 pounds of him. It took about thirty minutes, and I don't know how many times I had to remind myself of the Possibility Thinkers Creed.

The real point I want to make is that I think the greatest thrill of the week was not catching a marlin but having about three days with that spiritual giant, Dr. Bob Pierce. Now it's been my joy to know people like E. Stanley Jones, Billy Graham, Norman Vincent Peale, and I don't want to be an ecclesiastical name dropper, but Bob Pierce has got to be one of the great hearts of our time. Nobody has done more to create orphanages for homeless children than Bob Pierce. In my mind he is one of the greatest success stories of the century.

There was a very touching scene for me an hour before we left to come back home. Bob Pierce, who had been quite ill and was not expected to live more than a few months, was lying on his back in his bed. His friend Chuck Walters came in while I was there and said, "I won't say good-bye, Bob. I'm going to believe that you are going to live longer than they think you will." With a radiance on his face and a serenity that can only come from the presence of Jesus Christ deep within him, Bob said, "You know, I've been talking with my Lord here in bed the last few minutes. There just isn't anybody in the world that I feel I have to go to and make amends with as I come to the end of my life. And that's a good feeling." Bob and I talked about this through the week. I told him, "Bob, you have a great attitude." "I feel beautiful," he told me. "I really do. I gave my life to Christ and that's the best thing I ever did. Now in coming to the end, I feel good."

Dr. Bob Pierce can face the end of his life with pride behind him. Wouldn't you feel great if tens of thousands of orphans and hundreds of thousands of starving people were given life because God used you? He comes to the end of his life with *pride behind him, love around him and hope ahead of him.*

His ministry started back in Amoy, China, in 1947, when one of our missionaries over there came to Dr. Pierce one day with an eleven-year-old girl. "Take her," she told him, "I've got four adopted ones of my own and I can't take another one. You want to be a minister? You want to be a missionary? You want to do something? Here. Feed and clothe this little girl." And that was the beginning of World Vision. That was the beginning of what turned out to be Bob Pierce's great ministry throughout Asia and the world.

What I'm trying to say to you is that in your goal setting, begin with problem solving possibility thinking. *With God it's possible!* Then begin with your value system. Set your values in tune with God and with His Word to make sure that if you succeed you'll be proud of it. And if you fail, you will be proud of your failure, too, because you will know at least, that you tried to do something beautiful for God!

3. *Aim at growth in quality and quantity.*

Avoid the cop-out trap of saying, "We're not growing in numbers but we are sure growing in quality." If you really improve in quality, you're going to improve in quantity, unless you've saturated the market with your product. That means, then, if you aim in your goal setting, you look for growth-restricting areas. What is restricting the growth of our company or *your own personality?* Leadership looks for growth-restricting obstacles and sets goals accordingly. Leadership develops possible ways in which growth-restricting obstacles can be corrected so that the individual or institution can grow as large as it can become.

Ask yourself, "Is there some area where we haven't been growing? Is there some department where we haven't been making progress?" And if your plant or equipment is limiting your growth and development, develop more plants and equipment. If capital is limiting your growth and expansion, then you know you have to increase capital.

4. *Look at and study very carefully your prejudices, your passions and your concerns.*

Chances are, it will be in these areas that you will discover your blind spots. For your goal setting should aim at eliminating personal blind spots. And we all have them. In other words, if you feel very deeply and passionately on some prejudicial issue, I would advise you to look at it very carefully and just play a game and take the other side of the coin. Try putting yourself in the other guy's shoes. You may be led into an area of your emotional life where growth and maturity are deeply called for.

5. *Check the success potential before you set your goals.*

You can almost always check whether an idea will be a failure or a success before you begin asking, is it practical? Does it fill a vital human need? Can it excel? Can it inspire? Is it pace-setting? Can your idea really meet a need? Can it be inspirational? Can you package it in such a way that people will want it? Will it touch them emotionally? If you're the first with the most, you can't lose unless you don't have the nerve to move ahead.

6. *In setting goals, don't surrender leadership to problems.*

Keep a positive attitude toward problems when you set your goals. Never bring the problem-solving phase into the decision-making phase. Don't let your problems take command; let possibilities take command. The decision-making phase should always be separated from the problem-solving phase. You make the decision, then you solve the problem. Most people fail because they don't make the decision until they solve the problem. If you don't make the decision until you solve the problem, by the time you make the decision somebody else will have done it ahead of you. Furthermore, most problem-solving and creative thinking never happens when you're in a phase of indecision. When you make the decision—make the plunge because it's a great idea and it would help God and other people! Then you know you've got to sink or swim. In that kind of situation, the breakthrough ideas will come.

In all of your goal setting, *let your goals become targets but never let them become ceilings. If your goals are not expandable they will be expendable.*

Let me illustrate. Our first church was built on only two acres of land in another part of Garden Grove. I could see that the church could grow only that large in that location and then it would be non-expandable. We wouldn't be able to park the cars. If the goal is not *expandable* it is *expendable*. Because then the time will come when you're choked and you can't grow. And what will happen then? Dynamic, creative staff people will drift away. Dynamic creative people can only work in companies, corporations, institutes and situations where there is constant challenge, and replacing them will be the kind of people who don't want to take chances, who don't want to pay high prices and who want to take it easy. That will be the new leadership. And even a dead fish can float downstream. *If the goal is not expandable it is expendable!*

7. *Let the size of your God set the size of your dream.*

In other words, make your goals big enough for God to fit in.

Remember, you can never do anything by yourself. If you are a success it will only be because *others made you successful!* It is your responsibility to set your goals—God will use *others* to make them come to pass! That means you begin by drawing support first of all from God Himself. I don't believe that any person will be a happy success without God.

I want to ask you one question: Are you happy with the goals you've set for yourself? If not, you're free to set new goals. Don't tell me you're too old. Don't tell me you don't have the money. Don't tell me you don't have the connections, the brainpower or the willpower. That's locked-in thinking. Assuming that there is a solution to every problem, what goals would you set for yourself today? Where are your priorities?

Let me ask you this: How is your relationship with God? You don't want to set any goals unless your heart is right with God. He says to you, *"I have set before you life or death, blessing or curse. Oh, that you would choose life."* Your first priority should be *to choose life*—life centered on God and filled with the presence and power of the Savior, Jesus Christ. That's where the successful life begins. That's where you must begin, also!

# Discover Freedom

# 1

## Chains? Or Change?

Have you ever felt chained to a bad habit or a negative thought process? Perhaps you're bound by a problem or by unending frustration and you long to be free. Listen to these beautiful words of Jesus:

"You will know the truth and the truth will make you free!" (John 8:32).

Chains? Or change? Only you can make the choice! It's incredible what freedom there can be for you from whatever may be binding you today. But in order to understand the truth that can set you free, you must first ask the question: What did Jesus mean when he said, *"The truth shall make you free?"*

What is "the truth" that allows change to break the chains? To answer that question I must first ask four additional questions:

1. What is your great need?
2. What is your biggest obstacle?
3. What is your deepest desire?
4. What is your only salvation?

If you ask the right questions, you'll get the right answers. Get the right answers and you'll know the truth! *And the truth shall make you free!*

A few weeks ago I went to Beverly Hills to perform the marriage ceremony of a good friend of mine, Glen Ford. A small group of Hollywood friends were invited to Glen's home so I chatted with a few of them before the wedding. Among the celebrities were John Wayne, Jimmy Stewart and Frank Sinatra.

As we stood there and talked, one of them casually lit up a cigarette. Just as he took his first puff, Mr. Stewart turned to John Wayne and said, "Duke, when did you quit smoking and how did you quit?" John replied, "I quit when I decided that it was more fun breathing than smoking!" I think that's great!

The lungs are indispensable. You can get by without hands; you can get by without arms; you can get by without ears; you can even get by without a portion of your brain but you cannot get by without at least one lung, one kidney, a liver and a heart! Take care of your body. Guard your health and enjoy healthy, abundant living!

Are you chained? If the desire to break your chains is strong enough, they can be snapped. You are not

bound by anything unless, at a deep level, you want to have that bondage. It is possible for the chains to be changed. *Your greatest need is to believe that it is possible!*

Since infancy, I have been addicted to something far stronger than cigarettes, heroin, or alcohol—Bad eating habits! Over-indulging in pies, cakes, pastries, cookies and ice cream has always been a weakness of mine. And any expert in behavioral modification will tell you that it is more difficult to break these life-long eating habits than it is to break cigarette smoking, narcotic addiction or alcoholism. Why? Because, from infancy, your emotional needs are subconsciously identified with your eating pattern. If you've lost a loved one you may eat rich foods because it touches some subliminal recollection of a good time you once shared with them. And for me that meant cake, ice cream, cookies and other fattening foods. I was hopelessly addicted to foods that I knew were making me overweight. And for the first time in my life, I realized that I could have a serious high blood pressure problem if I didn't change my eating habits soon. But it wasn't until six months ago, after eating a large meal in Orlando, Florida, that I asked God to help me.

I had returned to my hotel room, full of rich food. I went to bed feeling terribly guilt-stricken and awoke at 3 o'clock in the morning. Have you ever felt guilty about something you did? I can tell you that I have never committed fornication, nor adultery. I am faithful to my one and only wife and we have been happily married for 27 years. But honestly, if I had committed adultery, I could not have felt more guilty than when I awoke at 3 o'clock in the morning with food in my stomach that I knew was a sin for me. I knew that I was

hopelessly addicted so I went into a time of relaxation, meditation, and two-way prayer.

In a matter of seconds I can get myself in such a state of relaxation where I am not at all conscious of my body weight, but sense that I am floating suspended in space. And this is when I go into two-way prayer. I cried out from the depths of my heart. "Jesus Christ, I believe in you! I preach about you. I think you are the Son of God. But I've never touched you. Maybe I've just been indoctrinated, maybe it's all just a trick. If you

are there, you know about this problem I have. Can you help me?"

And in an instant, I had a vision. I saw in my mind's eye a river—flooded over its banks. The water looked so safe that a baby could wade in it. Why, it was as safe as a piece of bread and a pat of butter. The water was so calm, so harmless and so serene. Why, it was as safe as an ice cream cone on the way home from work. But then the water started moving downstream. It was no longer perfectly calm, but it still couldn't hurt me any more than one piece of pie. Then suddenly I saw white caps roaring out of control and at the heart of the flood waters was a gigantic tree that had been uprooted. My body was that dead tree!

Then I heard these powerful words, "I have snatched you from destruction!" I felt myself lifted like that broken tree and planted on safe ground. I felt like I was healed of a disease. I was at peace! Chains? There was a change! And I didn't do it, He did it! I have since, totally lost all appetite for these foods. I have an appetite for salads, vegetables, lean meats, fish and delicious fruit for dessert. (With the rare exception of a soufflé once in a while.)

My weight is down and my health is vibrant and vital! And Jesus gets the credit, I don't.

All I did was believe in the vision. I believed that it might be possible for a 50-year-old man to experience such a change.

Now, the sequel, as if God wanted to prove to me that it was not a trick in my mind, is unbelievable. Thirty days later, I was in a Japanese Hotel of all places. One afternoon I went downstairs to do some shopping. I asked the clerk what it would cost to ship a few things to America. Before she could reply, a man with an incredible Oxford accent said, "Why don't you check it through in your luggage?" I turned around and there was a black man with the most beautiful eyes.

When Jesus Christ was here on earth His eyes must have looked like this man's eyes. I was dumbfounded for a moment as I gazed at this black man with all his regalia. Later I found out he was a tribal chief from

Nigeria and an Anglican leader from that country. I looked at him after I caught my breath and said, "That's a good idea." Not giving me a chance to turn back to the clerk, he asked, "Are you lecturing here at the Congress?" "No," I replied, "I'm lecturing here in the churches. I'm a Christian." "So am I!" he enthused. "Oh," I exclaimed, "I thought I saw Christ in your life and in your eyes!" "Of course," he responded. "Can I tell you about it?"

Ignoring the stares from the clerk, he told me an incredible story. He began, "The days that I do not have a chance to share Christ, I count as a day lost in my life. You see," he explained, "I had a marvelous experience with Christ eight years ago." "Tell me about it," I urged. "I was very ill and had to go into the hospital for extensive tests." He continued, "I received the best care because I'm a tribal chief but I knew the doctors had bad news when they entered my room. With serious expressions on their faces, they told me I had very little time to live. They told me I was fatally ill and there was nothing they could do medically for me. My life span would be measured in weeks or months.

"I asked them if doctors in London could help and they said no. I even asked them if doctors in America might be able to help. But once again they said no. 'All we can do,' they said, 'is give you medication when the disease brings pain.' I was so discouraged, I asked them to leave the room and they graciously obeyed.

"Alone in my room, I looked up at the ceiling and I fervently prayed. 'Jesus, I have always believed in you.' (Almost the same prayer that I had prayed in Florida.) 'I have never touched you. Maybe it's all a big myth but if you are alive and if you can hear me now, can you heal me?' " (Incredible! I asked God to help me and he asked God to heal him!) Full of enthusiasm my friend continued with his story.

"I suddenly saw a vision. I saw a blanket, it was descending—floating, tattered and worn. I knew it was rotten and that if I tried to pick it up and fold it, it would have crumbled into dust. My body was that blanket. Then I heard a sentence that I know came from Jesus. 'I have healed you!' " The distinguished tribal chief said, "I mean with total belief, I knew that I was healed! I never doubted it, I knew it! It wasn't a matter of an act of faith, it was an experience of knowing. My recovery was immediate and complete. Look at me!"

We prayed together and then he went his way and I went mine. This wonderful person came into my life without invitation and he left with a smile. I never saw him before and will probably never see him again. But I know that God sent him to me, a half a world away, four weeks after Christ spoke to me in Florida, to break down any obstacles in this potentially critical mind of Schuller's. What happened to me was not a psychological trick, it was an authentic act of the living Jesus Christ!

Now, I cannot promise you that same miracle! But I can promise you this: No problem is too big for God's power and no person is too small for God's love. Don't ever say, "It's impossible!" Chains? They can be broken. There can be great change! You know your biggest needs, your greatest obstacle, your deepest desire and your only salvation.

Your biggest problem is yourself. You are the only person who can say, "It's impossible." What's the difference between a possibility and an impossibility? Quite simple. The difference is a person; an attitude; and two words. The person is you! The attitude is "I CAN." The two words are "I WILL." Your deepest desire is to love yourself. If you love yourself you will believe in God and you will think it's possible. Your only salvation is Jesus Christ who alone can heal and save and redeem. He wants to, He really does!

He is alive! Reach out for Him! He can touch you in His own way! He can save you right now!

# 2

## You Can
## Experience Freedom

"This is the day the Lord hath made, let us rejoice and be glad in it!" Are you rejoicing today or are you bound by worry and frustration? Don't make chains for yourself—CHANGE! *Experience freedom!* For Jesus said, "I have come to set the captives free."

Istanbul, once called Constantinople, is a beautiful city—one of the great cities in the world. When you enter the harbor by ship, as I did some years ago, it is an inspiring sight to see. You enter the Golden Horn and sail up the Sea of Marmara. From there you can catch the view of the sun reflected off the gold domes of the mosques that were originally built as great cathedrals. They were built over 700 years ago and they still stand today as glorious monuments to people and their faith.

There was a time in the ancient days when insecure rulers of Constantinople wanted to make sure that they could keep the enemy out of their harbor. As a result, they performed a remarkable feat. They created the largest and heaviest chain ever built by human beings. The links are about a foot-and-a-half long and about two inches thick. This monstrous chain was draped across the harbor to keep foreign ships out of their territory. People still question how something that heavy could be maneuvered. We really don't know, but remnants of the chain can still be seen today.

Have you drawn a chain across the harbor of your mind? Most of us have a pretty good idea of what we believe but the thought of new concepts coming in is rather threatening. To have a chain across your mind

that can keep new thoughts from streaming in, that could unload a cargo of abundant prosperity to you, has to be one of the most foolish things you could do. Then why do you do it? Because you have made chains. The entrance to your mind is blocked just as the harbor of Constantinople was. You are given opportunities yet you can allow yourself to be bound. But you can break the chains and change!

## I. Some People Take Chains

How do people become bound by chains? By allowing themselves to believe negative thoughts that are put into their minds. Some people willingly take the chains and allow themselves to be bound. Other people make their own chains and are responsible for their own slavery. Some people take chains, some people make chains, and some people *break* chains!

The Bible says: *"God has not given us a spirit of fear, but of faith, and love and a sound mind."* God does not give us a spirit of doubt. God does not give us the spirit of anxiety and worry. God does not give us negative thoughts. They do not come from God. You want to make a change? You have to snap the chains of negative thinking—that chain of negative thoughts. One chain leads to another, one link leads to another, one negative thought leads to another. Fear produces anxiety, anxiety produces insecurity, insecurity produces a lack of courage and you have a whole negative-thinking cycle going. It's tragic!

But you have a choice! Chains or change? God is love and He wants to snap the chain and bring a wonderful change in your life. Max Scheller said: "Love is becoming aware of the highest possibility inherent in someone." If love is becoming aware of the highest possibility in someone, then who can love that way? Can you? No. Can I? No. None of us are really capable of understanding the highest possibility inherent in a person. Only God can love like that! He is love! No wonder we sing, "Jesus loves me this I know, for the Bible tells me so." Love is becoming aware of the highest possibility inherent in a person. Jesus sees great possibilities—the highest possibilities in you and in me and in everyone!

But you are never going to change into a happy, joyful, abundant person until you snap the negative thinking habit; until you stop accepting and nourishing negative thoughts. You can't move in the right direction until you change your thinking. Glen Cole, a graduate of our Institute for Successful Church Leadership, and pastor of a church in Washington, told me a story the other day that illustrates this. He boarded an airplane and sat next to a professional basketball player whom he recognized right away. Before the plane ever took off, my friend started asking the young man some questions. A basketball player in his younger days, Glen turned to the athlete and said, "When you are guarding a player what do you look for? What do you really watch? Do you watch his eyes? Do you watch his hands? Or his feet?" If you will excuse my language I'd like to say it the way he did, "I only keep my eye on his belly button, because until it moves he isn't going anyplace!"

I have met many people all over the world who can put on a good show but until they change their thinking, they aren't going anyplace. They may have lots of style

but their thinking is what really makes the difference. Some people take chains, and because of their thinking style they allow themselves to be bound. I was born into a poor family. We had no electricity—we couldn't afford it. We had kerosene lamps! I don't remember getting gifts at Christmastime. We went to church and I got some candy in Sunday School. I know what poverty is and my heart goes out to many of you who have known nothing but poverty in your lifetime. I'm here today to say that you can change! Whether you inherit poverty, oppression or prejudice you don't have to take it! I'll tell you why. Because you are a child of God! And he can break the chains!

One of the greatest men in Judea today is a Palestinian who was educated in Cambridge and returned to Jerusalem to establish his own business. Musa Alami did quite well by his standards until the political upheavel. He had to vacate Jerusalem and live in a refugee camp along with a lot of other poor Palestinian refugees. But rather than take that kind of a static, nonproductive life-style he decided to be a possibility thinker.

He stood on the top of a mountain and gazed on the hills of Moab. He saw only one trickle of blue flowing in the vast wasteland—the Jordan River flowing from Galilee to the Dead Sea. With all that desert, Musa thought, "If only there was more water." Then he came up with an incredible and impossible idea. "Why not dig for sub-surface water?" He had studied how someone in California dug for sub-surface water and succeeded! (Some of you Easterners don't know it, but California used to be pure desert.) Some persistent adventurers

dug deeper and deeper until they struck sub-surface water. That's why California is so green.

So, Musa talked to his friends about digging for water but their response was: "That's impossible! There is
no sub-surface water. Look at the barren hills of Judea,
there is nothing there. Look at the hills of Moab, there
is no snow there. The only snow is at Mt. Hermon and
that only feeds the Jordan River. There is no sub-
surface water, for there are no hills with snow-capped
glaciers." But Musa didn't listen to his friends. He re-
fused to believe in anything other than what he be-

lieved! Even though he had no money or equipment he began to dig. He and a few other poverty stricken refugees from the Palestinian camp went out one day with some picks and shovels and they started to dig a hollow in the sand. You can imagine that!

"You fools!" their friends mocked. "There is no water in Jordan!" But Musa and his companions kept on digging—one month, two months, three months, six months! Then one day they reached a point where the sand felt cool and changed colors. Could it be water? Then they dug a little deeper and found the sand to be moist. One more shovel full and the water began to seep in, covering the dry soil. They struck an underground river that had been there tens of thousands of years since the creation of this earth. When an Arab shiek finally heard the news he lifted up his long white gown and ran on sandaled feet to the place where Musa had been digging. "Is it really water?" he cried out. "I must see it and touch it and taste it!" And he reached down and splashed the water on his face! He cupped his hands and drew the refreshing water to his lips. His leathery, and tawny face broke out in wrinkles of smiles.

"Musa, you have found water! Now you can die— which was the shiek's way of saying, 'You have done something worthwhile in your lifetime, therefore you can die and know that your life has not been a waste.' " That was the beginning! Musa dug another well and another and another. Today he lives on a farm 3 miles wide and 4 miles long. He grows figs, citrus and vegetables! Not only that, but he was such an inspiration to

others that today there are now more than 40,000 acres blooming with super productivity!

Somebody said, "There is no water." And everybody told the next generation, "There can be no well." Everybody believed the negative-thinking experts! They were bound by the negative-thinking chains. Don't just accept chains. Don't take it—you don't have to! The thing that makes you different from the animals is that you are a decision-making creature. Some people just make their chains, they don't inherit them, they aren't born in poverty, but they make it for themselves. They are given an education, they are given opportunities but somewhere along the line they are their own worst enemy!

## II. Some Persons Make Chains

During the national league playoffs this year, the Los Angeles Dodgers played Philadelphia. My friend, Burt Hooten was pitching. There were two outs and two strikes against the batter when he pitched the next ball. Burt was so sure that it was a strike but the umpire called it a ball. That made him furious, and of course, the Philadelphia crowd loved it! The fans went crazy! Showing your feelings at an away game is like dropping blood in shark infested waters. Burt was really rattled. He walked the next four batters. But do you know what he told the press? "Some pitchers are knocked out by batters; some pitchers are taken out by an umpire; but the crowd didn't knock me off that mound, and the lineup didn't knock me out, only one guy knocked me out. Hooten booted Hooten out! I learned a lesson that every professional has to learn again and again. Only we can knock ourselves out!"

Don't make your own chains. So you've got a problem, things are going bad—you are the only one who can decide what it will do to you!

### III. Some People Break Chains

Don't take chains! Don't make chains! Break chains! Yes, some people *break* their chains. How do you break them? You break them by beginning to believe in what you can become. And how do you do that? By meeting Jesus Christ. Love is becoming aware of the highest possibility inherent in someone. That is what Jesus Christ does for you and that's what he did for me.

I was just a little boy on an Iowa farm when I began to believe that maybe I could make it a better world. What a ridiculous and impossible idea—that if I became a follower of Jesus Christ and a minister that the world would be a better and more beautiful place? I'm succeeding now and so will you if you let Jesus Christ come into your life. Listen to his voice.

The masses by nature, think negatively. The masses, by nature, will put you down. Jesus's voice is very different. He doesn't run with the herd, Jesus stands on the hill and He voices a lonely call. He says to you: You put yourself down, people put you down, but I believe in you! You are a plan waiting to unfold. You are a dream waiting to materialize. You are a brilliant idea waiting to become incarnate. You are an exciting concept of God waiting to be born again. Follow Him and productivity will astound you! Listen to His voice and He will choose and call you to great service.

Do you know where Arabian horses come from? They are such spectacular, gorgeous creatures. Legend says that the prophet Mohammed decided that he wanted to breed the finest horse on planet earth, so he searched the world over for one hundred striking mares. After he collected one hundred beautiful animals, he led them to the top of a mountain where he corralled them. Directly below them was a cool mountain stream which they could only see and smell. He deprived them of water until they were wild with thirst. Only then did he lift the gate, allowing all one hundred beasts to take off madly for the water.

All you could see were thundering, stampeding horses with tails flying in the wind, necks arched, nostrils flaring and mouths foaming, pulling themselves through clouds of spraying sand. Just before the stampeding herd reached the water, Mohammed put a bugle to his lips and blew with all his might. All of the horses kept on running except for four mares who dug their hoofs into the sand and stopped. With mouths foaming and necks trembling, they froze, waiting for the next command. "Those four mares will be the seeds of my new horse," Mohammed cried out! "And I will call them Arabian!"

A common person becomes uncommon simply because he or she hears a different bugle call! Listen to

Christ's trumpet and He will call you to greatness. Chains will be broken and the change will be beautiful. And you will experience the exhilarating feeling of freedom!

# Bloom Where
# You Are Planted

# 1

## The Person
## Makes The Place!

The place does not make the person; the person makes the place. That important life principle is based on one of my favorite verses in the Bible—Philippians 4:11. St. Paul writes:

"I have learned, in whatever state I am, to be content."

To put it in modern English, St. Paul is saying:

"I have learned how to be rich, how to be poor, how to be at comfort and how to take persecution. I have lived and walked with God, and I have learned that in whatever state of conditions or circumstances I find myself, I will not complain! I will make the best of it, confidently, and expect good things to come."

He practiced this principle! When he was thrown into prison, he bloomed where he was planted and produced what are now called the Prison Epistles.

Right now, you may be in a state of affairs, or in circumstances that you wish didn't exist. Well, just as you cannot tell a book by its cover, neither can you tell circumstances by their appearance.

I recently heard about a young man who was dashing through the airport to catch his plane. He was late, but as he passed the bookstore, he saw out of the corner of his eye a book entitled *How to Hug*. Being a very energetic young man, eager to win and influence his girl-friends, he quickly ran into the store, bought the book, eagerly anticipating reading it. Puffing passionately, he got on the airplane, opened his book on *How to Hug* and discovered he had purchased volume 12 of an encyclopedia! You just can't tell a book by its cover!

When I was growing up, I always thought that old women looked old, middle-aged women looked middle-aged, young girls looked young and little girls my age, well, they were just pretty and interesting. But today, times have really changed. You look at women today and they just don't show their age, and few of them really have had any face-lifting done. I don't know why this is, but it's really true.

I saw a woman not long ago who had to be about 80 years old, but she didn't look more than 50. I said to someone near me, "How old is she?" The fella said, "I don't know, but her Social Security number is four!"

*You just can't tell a book by its cover.* You just can't look at your situation or your circumstances and say, "I'm in a good spot," or "I'm in a bad spot." If you think that way, you're thinking wrong. *Every spot can be a good spot if God is in it!* It's that simple. It's not something you know by nature, it's something you have to learn. It's a mark of maturity.

This summer we flew in our travels to visit churches and mission stations. Our trip took us over the Tigris-Euphrates Valley to the desert plains of Persia, and I was reminded of a story that came to me in full force with a renewed recollection when we were in Teheran.

The Crown Jewels of Persia are kept in Teheran in a very highly protected place, as are all the Crown Jewels of monarchs.

I have seen the Crown Jewels of England; they are in the Tower of London. I have seen the Crown Jewels of the Czar and Czarina of Russia; they are in the Hermitage Museum, in Leningrad. I have seen the Crown Jewels of many of the great kings of the centuries, but I have never in my life seen anything that comes close to the Crown Jewels of Persia. They defy description, and form, literally, the international banking collateral for that country.

Undoubtedly, the most beautiful crown ever fashioned for the head of a human being, is the crown that was designed for the present Princess of Iran—to be worn at her coronation. As I looked at the huge silver tray overflowing with diamonds, I whispered to our guide, "Where did all these diamonds come from?" He answered, "Many of them come from the marvelous Golcanda mine."

The Golcanda mine is where the Kohinoor diamond came from, which is in the Crown Jewels of England, and the Orloff diamond, which is in the Crown Jewels of Russia. The story of that mine was made famous in our country years ago by Russell Comwell's book, *Acres of Diamonds*.

Once there was a man named Ali Hafed, who lived in the beautiful country of Iran. He was a farmer, and was content in his state of affairs. His farm was good and fruitful. He had a wife and children and raised sheep, camels and wheat. "If a man has a wife, sons, camels, health and the peace of God," Ali Hafed often said, "He is rich!"

Ali Hafed was rich until one day a priest came to visit and began talking about a strange thing the priest called "diamonds." Ali Hafed had never heard of diamonds. The priest said, "They sparkle like a million suns. They are the most beautiful things in the world!"

Suddenly, Ali Hafed became very discontented with what he had. He asked the priest, "Where can you find these diamonds? I must have them." The priest answered, "They say they can be found all over the world. Look for a white stream that flows through white sands surrounded by high mountains, and you'll find diamonds."

So Ali Hafed made a vow, sold his farm, left his wife and children in the care of a neighbor and set out on his journey to find diamonds.

He traveled through Palestine, then along the Nile

Valley, until finally he found himself at the Pillars of Hercules, entering the country of Spain. He looked for white sands, tall mountains, but found no diamonds. With years passing, he came one day to the coast of Barcelona, Spain, broken, destitute and unable to communicate with his family. In a fit of despair and utter defeat, he plunged into the sea and died.

Meanwhile, the man who bought his farm spotted an odd black chunk of rock while watering his camel one day. He took the rock home, put it on his mantel and thought nothing more of it.

Stopping in one day, the priest looked at it and saw a flash of color from a crack in the rock. He said to the man, "A diamond! Where did you find it?"

The farmer said, "I found it by the cool sands and white stream where I water my camel."

Together, lifting their robes and running as fast as their sandaled feet would carry them, they rushed to the stream. They scratched and dug and found *more* diamonds! That discovery became the Golcanda Diamond Mine—the greatest diamond mine in the world!

The lesson is obvious. Diamonds were in Ali Hafed's own backyard all the time. But he didn't see them. Instead, he spent his lifetime in a fruitless search!

The moral is also obvious. You can spend your lifetime in all kinds of travels and pursuits of pleasure, fame and wealth—all in an effort to find happiness. But happiness can be found under your own feet, in your own backyard. Bloom where you are planted!

Wherever you are, God is. Wherever God is, there are beautiful plans—if only you will see the possibilities. God put you where you are because He can see diamonds in the rocks all around you.

# 2

## *The Person Makes Success!*

If you were to list the names of the towns and cities wherein the greatest personalities in history have lived, I am sure most of you would list Rome, London, New York, Washington, Tokyo or Hong Kong. But the biggest people, on whom history hinged, did not live in those towns. Consider Cyrus the Great. Persepolis was his headquarters! Jesus of Nazareth—Bethlehem and Nazareth! Ghandi—the streets of India! Go on down the list of history, and what does it prove?

It proves that success and greatness does not depend on the place: *It depends on the person!* The place does not make the person; the person makes the place! That's what is so exciting. Power, success and achievement will come to you anywhere you are if your attitude is right.

The lesson is this: It's not *where* you are, but *what* you are that matters. And that's why the people whose lives have blossomed most fragrantly in human history often appear to have set up their headquarters in obscure cities, and the cities have become famous because they were there.

How do you bloom where you are planted? By thinking of the possibilities! Look at the possibilities under your feet right now, whatever your situation.

Not long ago I read about an elderly man who was known in his lifetime to be very rich because he was so thrifty—almost to the point of being considered a miser. When he died, it was discovered that in his room he had gallon cans filled with nickels. The bank examiner reported that the man saved most of his money and used it to put young needy men through college. That was why he was so thrifty! "That explains why he always looked so happy and contented," his neighbors remarked. It was also discovered that after he retired, each day he would fill his pockets with nickels and make it a ritual to walk down the streets of the business districts looking for cars whose parking meters had expired. When he found one, he would drop in a nickel! Now there was a happy man.

Bloom where you are planted. There are acres of diamonds under your feet right now—diamonds of joy, happiness and purposefulness in life. All you need to discover them is a dynamic, positive attitude.

Here in California we have many Army bases, and during the Second World War many of our young men were trained on them. One of these bases is located in a bleak, remote section of the desert.

There is a story of one young soldier who brought his wife out with him to this desert outpost. They wanted to be together as much as possible before he went overseas. The only housing they could find was an old shack that had been abandoned by the Indians.

For the first few days, the wife found it tolerable, and even rather pleasant. She and her new husband were together. But days added to days and the hours became long, lonely and boring. Then the winds came, and the sand storms struck and the heat went up over 115°. To her, the situation became intolerable!

When her husband was assigned to spend two weeks deeper in the desert, she reached the bottom of her negative, lonely attitude. She wrote her mother, saying:

"Mother,
   I'm coming home. I can't stand it here."

Within a week, she received a letter back from her mother with only these lines:

"Dear Daughter,
Two men sit in prison bars.
One sees mud, the other stars.
                    Love,
                    Mother"

She read the lines over and over again, until she became ashamed of herself. That night she thought, "I wonder what the stars look like from here." She went out of her shack and discovered what many Californians knew—in no other place in the world do the stars shine brighter than over the deserts of California. She thrilled to the beauty of the stars.

The next day she decided to take a walk, to explore her community. She walked down the road to the Indians who lived in shacks not far from her. They had never spoken, and she was certain the Indians were hostile and unfriendly. But she began talking to two women who were weaving. When the Indian women saw the woman was friendly, they became friendly. When she stopped *thinking* they were hostile, they stopped *being* hostile. Before she knew it, she was learning how to weave baskets.

One day several little Indian boys brought her seashells and told her the legend of how long ago the desert was the ocean floor. She became intrigued and started to collect sea shells in the desert. She was fascinated!

By the time her husband finished his assignment at that base, she had become such an authority on the desert that she had written a book on it! She fell in love with the desert and wept when she had to say good-bye to the most beautiful friends she had ever had—the Indians.

Bloom where you are planted. I have learned that in whatever circumstance, condition or place I find myself, with the help of God, I can turn it into a garden. It's possible, if you keep a happy, positive attitude. You will begin to bloom when you exercise a deep beautiful faith that God didn't make a mistake when he put you where you are!

I want to share with you one of the most beautiful letters I have ever received:

"Dr. Schuller,
Three years ago, I admitted myself to Bethesda Mental Hospital in Denver, Colorado, for two and a half weeks. It was the most beautiful experience of my life. I thank God for it. When I was there I wrote these lines, and I want to share them with you. I'm not a poet, and the rhyming may not be right, but it comes from my heart.

> 'I walked through the doors;
> They slammed shut behind me.
> There was nothing but sadness
>     and gloom.
> My mind was a blank, I didn't
>     give a—
> But there was nothing else I
>     could do.
> They put me in a room with two
>     other women;
> We stared at each other and
>     glared.
> They were blue, depressed and
>     numb just as I
> But mostly plain scared.
> "What would happen to us? Did
>     anybody care?
> Why are we here, in this room
>     bleak and bare?
> Please God, what will happen
>     to us."

'There were people there from
all walks of life;
A preacher, a teacher, a Colonel, a racer,
a salesman, secretary, house-
wife, baker.
But the saddest of all were the
young folks on dope.
For them I saw not a glimmer of
hope.

'The thing that made such an
impression on me,
Was something I heard, it was
almost a plea:
Walk tall, my friend, walk tall.
No matter how down and out
you may be,
No matter what fate has in store
for thee,
You've got to be true to your-
self, my friend,
Before you walk out that door.

'Oh yes, I was in a mental hos-
pital, my friends,
But things are looking up instead
of down.
My head's in the air, not down
on my chest;
A smile has replaced the frown.
It was hell, it was heaven, all
rolled into one.
Let me be the first one to say,
I thank God on my knees today.
He gave me the privilege to send
me that way.
"When you're so discouraged,
And life's a bad scene.
When suicide seems the only
way out,

Look, breathe deep, God won't
let you fall.
Just remember the words, walk
tall, walk tall!" ' "

Wherever you are today, there are great possibilities. There are diamonds under your feet, believe me. Your life can bloom wherever you are if you will think positive and try positively to help someone around you. Get interested in someone else who's hurting.

There was a ship that had sailed from the Orient coming up around the coast of South America. It had been a long voyage and the territory was new to the captain and his crew. They misjudged their water supply, and soon, off the coast of South America, they ran out. The entire crew was threatened with death from lack of water.

Fortunately, a passing ship flying a South American flag came by, and the distressed vessel signaled, "Can you share your water?" The passing ship signaled back, "Dip where you are."

The distressed captain thought it was an insane command and repeated his request. Again, the signal came back, "Dip where you are."

So a bucket and rope were lowered and the captain dipped into the salty ocean, lifted up a bucket of water, put his finger in it, touched his tongue and found the water was sweet. What he did not know was they were in the center of a mile-wide current in the ocean where the Amazon River was still making its surging inrush into the ocean!

Learn that in whatever state you find yourself, there are diamonds waiting to be mined. God put you where you are, and this week you're going to have a wonderful time living as you practice this faith!

# 3

## Opportunities
## Under Your Feet

I want to turn your attention to a Bible verse that, in a subtle way, really has a lot of inspiration in it. In writing to the church in Philippi, St. Paul adds in a closing verse this simple sentence:

"All the saints greet you especially those of Caesar's household" (Philippians 4:22).

Isn't that amazing? Even with all its viciousness, immorality and crime, there were Christians in the palace of Caesar!

How can *you* be a Christian in today's world? How can *you* be faithful to God Monday through Friday? *It's possible!* It's possible for people to be Christians to the point where St. Paul thought of them as *saints* in that unlikely place: *Caesar's household!* It's like saying that committed Christians have infiltrated the core of Communist cells in Eastern Europe! It's possible, for God has a way of scattering seeds so that they will bloom in the most unlikely places.

Bloom where you are planted. Your attitude—more than anything else—will determine whether you are a success or a failure.

J. W. Moran tells a story about visiting a friend and discovering some beautiful flowers pressed in his friend's old Bible. He neither knew the name nor the description of them, so he asked his friend who said, "These flowers were discovered on an expedition up a lonely, rocky promontory on the coast of New Zealand. My wife and I were exploring the region when we came across this terribly rocky stretch that probed out into the ocean. There, in the most unlikely collection of rocks, was this profusion of blooming wild flowers. What they were and where they came from we did not know; we were mystified to see them blooming in such an unlikely place! Evidently a seed blew in from a passing steamer, and it found its way into that little crevice, because the flowers are found in no other place in New Zealand. We were so inspired that we cut them, brought them home and pressed them."

Flowers in a rocky promontory! Saints in Caesar's household. Bloom where you are planted. Chances are, right under your feet, wherever you are, there is a beautiful opportunity—now!

I am reminded of an experience I had while visiting New Zealand last summer. I was told that one of the wonders of the world is the existence of the caves in Waitomo, one hundred miles north of Auckland, New Zealand. Once, they tell me, there was a farmer who owned the place, then sold it, not knowing that right under his land was one of the eight most beautiful wonders of the world!

In no place in the whole world can you see caves like you see here. You make your way down into the earth, walking the damp, dark hallway, holding onto an iron rail until you come to what is an underground river. Here you are told to get into a little boat and "not to utter a sound." You float down this underground stream, through underground caverns, to see a sight of amazing beauty. The guide who handles the little boat does not want to disturb the source of the living colors you are about to see, so he does not even paddle the boat. He quietly places his hands along the side of the damp canyon underground and nudges the boat slowly through the thick, inky darkness. The blackness is *solid*, total!

Suddenly you spot a billion sparkling little lights. For a moment you think you are in the desert on a clear night and seeing the Milky Way right above you! (You have lost all sense of perspective there in the dark tunnel!) The lights are really only four feet above your head! And what you see are the glowing lights of millions of glowworms that live in the caves! Twinkling, glowing like a million little neon lights, you can now hear—if you are very still—the chorus of the buzzing of these beautiful creatures.

Once God said to Moses, "Moses, what is in your hand?" Moses answered, "A rod." God must have smiled and said, "Ah, but don't underestimate that rod."

What's under *your* feet? What's in *your* hand? I want to give you four very simple but very workable tips that will help you to bloom where you are. I believe you can be a flower in a craggy wall or a saint in Caesar's household. I believe you can be a positive thinker in a world of negative thinkers or a shining light for Jesus Christ in a colony of people who despise you.

1. *Think positively.*

To bloom where you are planted may test your positive thinking to the limit. But do try to *think positively constantly*. Remember this principle: There's a *purpose* for every *place* and every *person* under the sun. *God has a purpose for every person in every place.*

Let me give you a short, simple sentence that will help you:

---

### GOD HAS NO WASTEBASKETS

---

God doesn't believe in waste! There's nothing that, in His mind, has to be thrown away as worthless!

I recently read a story in a hotel room in Tokyo.

"There was a Chinese wife who said to her husband, 'I would like a new coat.' Her husband said to her, 'What will you do with your old coat?' She answered, 'I will make a bed cover out of it.' He said, 'What will you do with your old bed cover?' She replied, 'I will make pillowcases out of it.' He asked, 'What will you do with the old pillowcases?' She responded, 'I will make new cleaning cloths' He said, 'What will you do with the old cleaning cloths?' She said, 'I will tie them together and make a mop out of them.' He continued, 'What will you do with the old mop?' She said, 'I will chop it up into little pieces, mix it with cement, and in the springtime we will patch the holes in our cottage.' He said, 'All right. You may have a new coat!' " If an Oriental can find a good purpose and use for everything—what can God do?

Dr. Henry Poppen, who spent forty years in China, once said to me, "We didn't throw away anything in China. We *even used ashes!*" I discovered this during my trip to Korea. In Korea they use ashes to fill the pockholes in the streets! *Nothing is wasted.* (More than one American has been embarrassed after travelling through the Orient to find that when he gets home after a period of time he gets a gift from the hotel operator. In the package are the little things he threw in his wastebasket!)

God has no wastebaskets. He has a purpose for every place and every person under the sun. Think positively and start to bloom where you are.

2. *Believe the best about every situation.*

Look for the best in every place, and believe the best about every person around you. Negative thinkers believe the worst about the place, the person and the situation.

I read the other day about a very distinguished businessman on the Long Island commuter train going into New York City. An unshaven man in a shabby coat brushed close to him, bumped him in the chest and made his way to the door, about to get off at the next stop. As an afterthought the businessman felt his pocket and discovered that his wallet was gone. Just then the train stopped, the doors opened, and the businessman grabbed the shoulders of the fellow who had bumped into him. Captured, the grubby fellow turned around with a horrified, frightened and desperate look on his face. Suddenly he lunged forward, broke free from his coat, and jumped off the train! The doors closed! And the businessman was left holding the culprit's coat! Immediately he went through the pockets, expecting to find his wallet, but they were empty! He went on to his office where his wife called him later in the morning and said, "Oh, honey, you left your wallet on the dresser this morning." (No wonder that poor unshaven fellow was so scared when he was getting off the train! He thought someone was robbing or attacking *him!*)

That's how wars and divorces start, and that's how problems in corporations begin. Someone jumps to a negative conclusion, thinking the worst about someone else! The most dangerous person in the world is a negative thinker who puts two and two together. Believe the *best* about someone. Think positively! Believe the best about persons, positions and situations.

3. Now, *remember always to be a positive reactionary.*

It's not what happens to you but how you react to it that determines whether you will bloom where you are, or dry up and die where you are.

There was a man who was stricken with an illness that left him totally paralyzed. A friend who hadn't seen him for many years came to his bedside and was struck by the change in his countenance and personality that followed this lengthy illness. Looking at his beautiful face as he was resting in bed, the friend said, "Sickness and trouble really colors a personality, doesn't it?" The paralyzed man replied, "Yes, it does, and I decided that I would choose the colors and make them beautiful."

When you have a positive idea, *react positively!* A fear of failure could tempt you to react negatively. Don't allow the fear of failure to dominate your thinking. Here's how you can conquer it. You simply say, "I've got an idea. I think it may be a God-given idea. I don't know if it will be a successful or a non-successful idea, so I will become a researcher and an experimenter. I will try it. If I try it and it works—great! If I try it and my idea doesn't prove successful, I will have been a successful researcher! I will have found out what didn't work. *Researchers never fail!"*

4. *Now tackle your problems positively and creatively.*

You can follow steps one, two and three and still run into problems. Of course, problems can cause you to shrivel up instead of blossoming in success. The important thing to remember is: *every problem can be solved!* If you run across what seems to be an unsolvable problem, chances are you have not properly *identified* it. The hardest part of solving problems is to correctly identify them.

There is a leading automobile manufacturer in Detroit, Michigan, that has this letter on file:

"Dear Sirs:
I have one of your cars, and I have a complaint about it. My complaint is that the car runs fine, until I go out and buy vanilla ice cream. I know you may think I'm crazy, but I'm serious! I buy my family ice cream every night. If I buy strawberry, chocolate or nut ice cream, my car starts fine! But if I buy vanilla ice cream the thing won't start!"

The top echelon in this automobile company laughed about this letter. Then someone said, "I don't think we should laugh. Let's send one of our engineers out there to check it out."

So an engineer went out and got a motel room near this man's home. He went to the man's house, found that he was a college graduate and that he lived in a fine part of his community. Every night the man would say to his family, "What kind of ice cream shall I buy tonight?" The kids would make their choice, and he would go out and buy the ice cream flavor they wanted.

True enough, the car started fine, except when the man bought the vanilla ice cream. The engineer went along every night for over two weeks until he finally figured out the problem.

In this particular ice cream shop all the flavored ice cream was at the end of the store, while the vanilla ice cream was right at the entrance door. There was always a line of people waiting to buy the flavored ice cream, and never a lineup for vanilla. So when he bought vanilla ice cream, he was only in the store a couple of minutes—and when he bought flavored ice cream he was in the store ten minutes! The problem was not the flavor of ice cream—the problem was *time!* Now the case could be responsibly diagnosed!

The problem with the car was a vapor lock. The car vapor-locked every night, but the extra five or ten minutes' wait for the flavored ice cream was enough time for the vapor lock to disappear. When the engineer diagnosed the problem right, he was able to solve it. The hardest part of solving problems is to correctly identify them.

Here is the point. Some of you think your problem is, "I'm living in the wrong community." "I belong to the wrong company." "I'm married to the wrong man." "I'm married to the wrong woman." *I will tell you that in nine hundred and ninety-nine cases out of a thousand* you haven't correctly identified the problem. The real problem is *your attitude!* Your *negative* attitude!

Think positively, try positively, and tackle your problems positively and creatively.

*Trust God confidently.* You didn't ask to be born. Chances are you had nothing to say about your parentage, the color of your skin, your national origin, probably not even the fact you are living where you are.

But God has been guiding you. He has a plan for you. Philippians 1:6 says:

"And I am sure that He who began a good work in you will bring it to completion at the day of Jesus Christ."

Dare to believe that you can blossom for Jesus Christ—right where you are! *Trust God confidently!*

Someone with a problem is going to touch your life soon; someone with a problem that only Jesus Christ can heal, that only Christ can satisfy. *You* be the saint in Caesar's household. *You* begin to bloom where you are planted! God will use you if you will think and try positively.

Instead of tossing ideas and dreams into the wastebasket, *throw the wastebasket away and replace it with a tackle box*. Then *tackle* every problem prayerfully, trusting in God.

You can be confident that God wants every flower to bloom. He wants every seed to sprout. He wants every person to experience joy and peace! That includes *YOU!* Bloom where *you* are planted!

# Discover How Life
# Can Be Beautiful

# 1

## *Snap The Trap*

Do you ever feel trapped, like everything is closing in on you? If so, God says to you:

"For I know the plans I have for you. They are plans for good and not for evil, to give you a future and a hope. In those days when you pray, I will listen. You will find me when you seek me, if you look for me in earnest. Yes, says the Lord, I will be found by you, and I will end your slavery and restore your fortunes" (see Jeremiah 29:11-14).

I believe we have our finger on the pulse beat of many people in our country and in our world today. And I can ask, Why do you feel trapped? What has trapped you? Do you have that emotionally trapped feeling, where you feel you are trapped by a fear that you cannot shake, or a hurt that you cannot dispose of, or an anxiety that seems to stubbornly resist relief and healing?

Is it an emotional trap? Is it a discouragement that seems to recur again and again? Is it a persistent negative thought that, like a grumbling neighbor, refuses to move out of the community; who constantly stays there to haunt you and to knock at your door when you least welcome his unfriendly coming?

I know of people who feel trapped by their singlehood, others who feel trapped in marriage, others who feel trapped in a job or unemployment.

Is there a habit that has been holding you—smoking?

drinking? narcotics? God will snap open the trap! *"I will be found by you, and I will end your slavery and restore your fortunes."* Now that's God's promise, and I want to share with you that it really works!

Some of you have heard me report on the International Congress of Psychologists, in Paris, France, which Mrs. Schuller and I attended. This is an area of my continued study, constantly trying to assimilate and synthesize psychological truth with theological and scriptural truth. I shall never forget attending, at that conference, a specialized workshop on Behavioral Modification. Behavioral Modification is the attempt to take someone who has an established behavior pattern and permanently try to alter and change it. The chairman of that event despairingly said, "You know, it gets discouraging. We are psychologists, interested in Behavioral Modification, yet I look at us and I would say most of us probably smoke too much, drink too much, or eat too much. We are overweight, and we exercise and move around too little."

It reminded me of an old proverb that says, "How can you tell your neighbor how to take care of his vineyards when your own vineyards are untidy, unkempt, untrimmed, and unpruned?"

I can declare to you with total conviction, there is no psychologist, there is no psychiatrist, there is no therapy in the world that can change human behavior like the Gospel of Jesus Christ and the power of God! Snap the trap! God can do it with your problem.

You may say, "But my problem is money. What can God do about that?" I remember coming out of a hotel in New York a few years ago. The cab drivers were all lined up and I had to pick the first cab. I will never forget the driver, not because of the color of his skin, but because he had a gold ring in his nose, which is most extraordinary. He smiled at me through the window, leaped out of his cab, recognized me from my New York television appearances each week, and said "Dr. Schuller! Hour of Power! I never thought I'd meet you in person. You changed my life!" (I watched the gold ring wriggle in his nose!) My cab driver continued, "Dr. Schuller, you transformed my life." He was so happy and joyful as he told me his story, a very pitiful story that could be multiplied a hundred thousand times in every city today in America. "I was born and raised in Harlem on welfare. I dropped out of school when I was 16 and in the 8th grade.

"One Sunday morning my wife and I were flipping the television dial and there you were, waving your hands and looking happy, talking about anything being

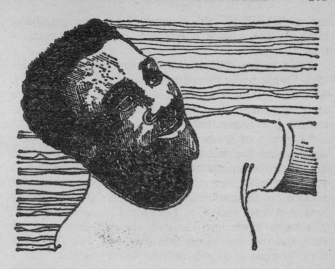

possible. I said to my wife, 'Sure, sure it's possible, if you're white and if you live in California by Disneyland.' She looked at me and said sternly, 'You know, I think your problem is exactly what he's talking about—you are an impossibility thinker. You are a negative thinker. You could get a job if you wanted to.' I got mad then and argued, 'That's not true. You know I want a job, but nobody will hire me. There's nothing I can do.' She said, 'You can drive a car; why not drive a cab?' I said, 'If I called them, the first thing they'd ask me is if I'm white or black. And when they find out I'm black, that kills it, you know that.' 'That's impossibility thinking,' she persisted. 'Try again.' So I picked up the telephone the next morning, called the cab company, and the first thing the man asked me was, 'Are you white or black?' I said, 'I'm black.' And he replied, 'Thank God! We need more black cab drivers in Harlem. The whites don't dare to drive here. You come down and you've got a job.' I went in, and I've been driving a cab ever since. We're saving money and we're going to buy our own little home. My wife, meanwhile, has gone back to school, inspired by your possibility thinking. She now is a secretary in a large organization."

I said to him, "What really turned you around?" He said, "What really turned me around that morning, Dr. Schuller, was when you told the story about those negative-thinking women in Louisiana." I didn't remember it so he reminded me:

"A group of women who lived on the bayou were complaining because they didn't live in the city and didn't have luxurious homes. One of the women was a positive thinker. She got so tired of the other complainers, the fault-finders, and the criticizers that she finally looked at them and said, 'Look, you live on the bayou. The bayou flows into the gulf, the gulf flows into the river and the river flows into the ocean. You've got a boat. You can go anywhere from where you are!' "

When you begin to believe in God, it's like having a house on the bayou. Because God, like the bayou, flows into the gulf, and the gulf flows into the river, the river flows into the ocean; and there's no end to the possibilities. So there is no end to God's power and God's possibilities to do something within you. And when you touch faith with God, it's like living on the bayou. You can go anywhere from where you are with the power of God, but you have to have a boat. You have to have belief. You have to have faith. And you have to take some action.

The good news I have for you is this: If you're trapped, the real reason you're trapped is YOU! Because being trapped is a feeling. To be trapped is an attitude. And who is responsible for your attitude? Others may be responsible for your condition, but you are responsible for your attitude. An attitude can liberate you or entrap you. Release can come to you if you will draw close to God. He has a plan for your life!

# 2

## Use The ABC's

How do you snap the trap! It's as simple as the ABC's.

A—*Ask* God what His plan is. Maybe you feel trapped, but maybe you are exactly where God wants you to be. Perhaps what you have to do is change your attitude toward the situation. You probably have been looking at your situation selfishly instead of from a service perspective. Perhaps God wants you there in order to share His love with others. You've looked at your job as just a job, but perhaps it's supposed to be used as a ministry. Maybe the reason you're working where you are is not because of the money but because of the ministry you could have. It's very possible that Jesus Christ would like to be working where you are, because the people around you need what Christ has to bring. You're not trapped; you've been liberated into an experience where you can change the little world around you. You could be exactly where you're supposed to be, but your attitude is wrong. God has a better plan and He's just waiting for you to ask and to pray.

Snapping the trap begins with prayer. He may leave you right where you are, but your attitude may change and everything could turn out great. I happen to be a deep believer in prayer and in Divine guidance. Ask!

B—*Believe*. When you ask, you will receive an answer. In Jeremiah 29:12 it says, *"When you pray, I will listen."* God will hear you. When you find God, it means you find His will for your life. Believe in the big, beautiful idea that unfolds in your mind. It will seem impossible—God's ideas are always impossible when they first strike us. If there were no obstacles, no problems, no risk of failure, it wouldn't require belief at all. Because belief is only exercising faith, and faith is taking a chance on something you can't prove. Ask! Believe!

C—*Commit* yourself to God's ideas when they come. Commit yourself to begin to do it. And commit yourself to continue to do it. This ties in with D . . .

D—*Discipline* yourself, because possibility thinking is never easy.

I happen to be a runner, and I'm proud of this. There have been some mornings when I didn't feel like running. In Paris this summer we stayed in the Hilton Hotel, and every morning I ran four miles at the base of the Eiffel Tower. When we went to Lucerne, where I wanted to do some writing, I thought, "Oh, I'm too tired to get up and run this morning. I'm going to luxuriate." But my conscience provoked me, and a voice said, "Schuller, you're 49. You'll soon be 50. The habits you form now you'll live and die with, and if you get into a bad or lazy habit and start letting down, you've had it. You're over the hill!" That scared me. I got up, put my running shoes on, went through the lobby of this luxurious, snobbish hotel and headed for the Lake of Lucerne. It was there that I had an experience I'll never forget.

I don't think I had been running a half mile when I met a man along the lake. They have a beautiful wide boulevard, where people can walk. There was a man who had two crutches, and one leg was amputated at the knee with the pant leg pinned back. He was hobbling on one leg with his crutches, as I came running along. He looked at me, like a hungry, starving child looking at a piece of bread—as if to say, "Oh God, I wish I could run."

Then God gave me what I call a "double whammy." If you've been to Lucerne, you know that the river comes into the lake and there's a bridge over it at that place. At that bridge was an old woman pushing her husband, an old man, in a wheelchair, and he had lost both his legs. He had that same look—like a starving child looking through a window at a fat man feasting on food. He watched me running with both legs. I'll tell you, did I run! I ran four miles that morning. I ran four miles the next morning in Washington. I ran four miles the next morning in Honolulu. I never missed a day in all that hopping and skipping around planet earth.

*Ask*—God's got a plan. *Believe*—you can do it even though you've never done anything like it before in your life.

Make a *Commitment*, because belief always calls for commitment. And commitment always leads to *Discipline*. And once you've disciplined yourself . . .

E—*Expect* a miracle! Because there will be a breakthrough when suddenly you know you're on top of it. The trap is snapped! You've been set free. Jesus Christ has helped you put down cigarettes, drinking, narcotics, the hurt, depression, or despair—and you'll look back and see it's like being converted. And maybe that's exactly what happened, because maybe you had never been converted before. You are born again! Praise God! Let Him snap the trap.

F—*Fly* high and free. When you get close to God, He promises, "I will end your slavery" and He says you will be free! It's like sailing on the bayou—there's no limit.

You can go anywhere with God from where you are!

# 3

## *Alter Your Altars*

I want to call your attention, again, to what I consider to be the key to happiness, truth and love.

"For I know the plans I have for you," says the Lord. "They are plans for good and not for evil, to give you a future and a hope" (Jeremiah 29:11).

God has a plan for your life and He has a plan for mine. Let me ask you this question: Are you really filled with happiness, hope, joy, courage and faith? If not, is it possible for your life to totally and completely reverse itself into a positive experience? The answer to that question is very important.

One of the significant questions raised at the International Congress of Psychologists, held in Paris, France, was this very same question. Can you totally, deeply transform and change human nature and character?

In the behavior modification seminar referred to earlier, a tremendous group of persons, most of whom were psychologists, were in the audience. The esteemed psychologist who was presiding over the group said, "We have to raise the question, can we really modify or change human character and behavior?"

I believe that every human being has an altar. An altar is that red button or that green button deep within yourself that causes you to be the person you are and causes you to react the way you react to almost every conceivable human situation. Now that is what I call your hidden altar, and that hidden altar is your command center. It is your power point.

I suggested, and I continue to suggest, that you can never change human nature unless you touch their but-

tons. Push the red button and POW! Push the green button and WOW! You and I have red and green buttons. And people change when you push the right button.

Now the problem of the typical, classical, rationalistic approach of the psychologist, psychiatrist and the average clergyman is that because we have been very well educated, we have become rational thinkers. We attempt to change people through the rational approach. But people never change from rationality, they only change when you touch their buttons—when they are turned on emotionally.

Alter your altars and your whole life will change. What do I mean by an altar? Every person has an altar. It is the control center deep within you—that source of emotional nourishment that turns you on or off. Your altar is the power plant that controls you. You may not even know it. You may not even be aware of what it is, but every person has a command center. Touch it and it sparks. Hit it and you hear things. The hidden command center, the control center, the power point, is your altar.

Now for some people it can be found in their ideology. You can look at some radical Maoists or Marxists and you will see what I mean. They hijack a plane, put bombs in lockers and think nothing of killing and terrorizing to try to achieve their objective. Their ideology is their altar.

In other cases a person's personal philosophy of life is his altar. It shakes his red button or his green button.

In still other cases it is the value system people live by. The value system may be power and the want of it. It may be recognition and the calling out and craving for it. It may be the satisfaction of pleasure.

I recently received a letter from Viktor Frankl, the esteemed psychiatrist, in Vienna, Austria. He shared with me these words: "I notice, having recently returned from America, that everybody there is on a pleasure kick. I declare to you that those who make pleasure their main goal in life are doomed to failure. This is because man is then no longer told by his driving instincts what he must do and he is no longer told by his traditional values what he must do. Those who no longer know what they want to do and have no purpose in life will fall victim to conformity, doing what others do, and pleasure and materialism will not fulfill them. Not ever."

Let's check your altars. Will your altars really bring you happiness, peace of mind and lasting joy? Or are they the source of your major aggravation, irritation, tension and trouble? Whatever you do, make sure that your altar doesn't alter you for the worse.

For some of you it's pleasure. Or you might find your altar in your value system. For some, it's money. Somebody once said the most sensitive nerve in the human body is the one that leads to the pocketbook.

In 1923, a very important meeting was held at the Edgewater Beach Hotel, in Chicago, Illinois. Attending that meeting were nine of the world's most successful financiers. Those present were the president of the largest independent steel company, the president of the largest utility company, the president of the largest gas company, the greatest wheat speculator, the president of the New York Stock Exchange, a member of the president's cabinet, the greatest "bear" on Wall Street, the head of the world's greatest monopoly, and finally the president of the Bank of International Settlements. It was what I would call a high-powered group of people. You must admit, they were men who knew the secret of making money. There was no doubt where their altar was.

Let's take a look at where they were 25 years later, in 1948. The president of the largest independent steel company, Charles Schwab, died bankrupt after living on borrowed money for his last five years. The president of the largest utility company, Samuel Insull, died a fugitive from justice, penniless in a foreign land. The president of the largest gas company, Howard Hopson, was insane. The greatest wheat speculator, Arthur Cutten, died abroad, insolvent. The president of the New York

Stock Exchange, Richard Whitney, had just been released from Sing Sing. The member of the president's cabinet, Albert Fall, was pardoned from prison so he could die at home—broke. The greatest "bear" on Wall Street, Jesse Livermore, died a suicide. The president of the Bank of International Settlements, Leon Fraser, died a suicide. *All of these men knew how to make money, but not one of them knew how to live!*

Check your altars. Are you sure where your heart is? Are you sure that the altar that controls your life is going to give you happiness, peace and joy further down the road you travel? Check your buttons!

# 4

## *Everything Can Change*

The exciting thing is that when you alter your altar, you alter everything. When you change your control center and your power center, everything changes.

One of the most exciting lectures presented at the International Congress of Psychologists was a fascinating report by Dr. H. E. Gruber, from the United States. He had made a study of the draft resisters in the United States during the controversial Viet Nam conflict. Dr. Gruber said he thought it would be interesting to study why some men became draft resisters, while others did not. He admitted, "Before I entered this study, I felt I knew what the answers would be. Obviously they would be persons of a particular political stripe, leaning toward the left rather than the right. Probably not conservative, but maybe politically liberal. I thought they would be of a certain emotional type. I knew that obviously they would have had a deep learning experience, perhaps indoctrination, or a traumatic psychological encounter which caused them to become such rigid draft resisters. I also was confident that I would find that they all tended to be reactionary and rebellious types who needed to stand aside from the crowd.

"The amazing thing is," he continued, "that when I had finished my study, I found I was wrong on every count. They didn't follow a political stripe. Some were conservatives, some were liberals. Some were very cold emotionally and some were very cuddly emotionally. So what caused them to become draft resisters? You will be most disappointed as psychologists to hear my answer, but I have to be honest with you. It was not some deep learning experience, it was not some traumatic emotional encounter. It was usually some apparently trivial thing.

"The case I'm about to give you is typical," he said. "One young man, who happened to be a politically conservative, emotionally stable, non-reactionary, non-rebellious type, was waiting for a bus. He went into a nearby drugstore and began browsing through the paperback books. He happened to pick up one book in particular and read a couple of pages. A couple of the lines grabbed him and caused him to think differently. When he put the book back on the shelf and walked out of the drugstore, he had made a turn around, even though he didn't know it yet. But," as Dr. Gruber said, standing on the platform addressing the assembly, "when he went out of that drugstore, emotionally and ideologically, instead of going one way, he went another and on down the line became a draft resister. The outcome, the difference in the destination, was tremendous." Something pushed one of his buttons.

Now how can you alter your altars? I can tell you one thing: *Nothing gives peace of mind like God!* Nothing fills you quite like Jesus Christ. You may perhaps be so successful and so intelligent that you think you're too sophisticated for God, but nothing satisfies like God.

For instance, let me share with you a letter that I

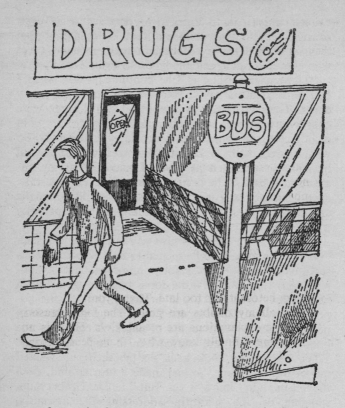

recently received from a psychologist here in Southern California:

"Dear Dr. Schuller, I have accidentally tuned in to watch bits and pieces of your ministry on Hour of Power over the past two years. I say accidentally because for most of my life I have been a professed, logical, close-minded atheist, which pains me to even write about at this point in my growth. But I was strong in my unbelief. In spite of my conviction, or lack of it, there was something about you and your television ministry that intrigued me. In spite of my hardheadedness and negative conceptualization of the state of man, I caught myself from time to time listening to you. You had a way of throwing peacefulness over those T.V. waves. What I'm really saying to you is that you brought a little glimpse of God into my life and I didn't realize it. At times I did realize it and struggled to resist God, but I couldn't win.

"Over the course of the past several months, I have been working on improving my life as a psychologist and everyone else I encounter. Without realizing it, I was preparing myself for a wonderful gift, because recently my wife and I were sitting in our living room and I had that religious experience. I know I was in the presence of God for a brief moment. Yes, me, the all-out unbeliever. He touched me, and it was like returning home, returning back to every person, place, experience and memory in my life that was beautiful and joyful. It was a sense of going home, mixed with grief, nostalgia, elation, release, great understanding and peace of mind. All I could say over and over again was, 'Thank you, thank you, thank you for letting me know You, God, before it was too late. Thank you!'

"Today all my doubts are gone. The logic, reason, and scientific explanations are meaningless. There is no more worrying. I finally know what I have been looking for for so long—it is peace of mind. And the most wonderful thing of all—faith in God. It is now 100 per cent."

Alter your altars! How does it happen? In strange ways, sometimes in little things. You come to church with a friend, not expecting anything, but something happens. We hear about it all the time. I can report to you that there is no psychiatrist, no psychologist or no behavioral scientist who has a greater, authentic, documentable record of changing people deeply, permanently or lastingly that we who minister in the name of Jesus Christ and in the power of God.

Do people really change? Can you alter your altars? You may say, "Well, maybe a good guy can become a better guy. But bad people, people intrinsically bad, don't suddenly change."

Some of you may remember Bill Sands, author of the

book, *My Shadow Ran Fast*. He was a friend of mine and we had his funeral services here in our church. He was such a tough crook that he was listed as incorrigible and not eligible for parole. He was sentenced to solitary confinement in Sing Sing. The warden at the time was a man named Duffy who believed he could transform persons through his Christian love. He believed that the worst person could be totally transformed and changed into someone beautiful, and he wanted to try to reshape Bill.

One of the chief executives and administrators in the prison had an argument with Warden Duffy, and they had a real headpounding, inter-office argument. Finally Mr. Duffy's opponent said, "Mr. Duffy, leopards don't change their spots." And Warden Duffy said, "I don't have any leopards in Sing Sing. I only have people. And people change." And as some of you know, Bill Sands was completely, totally and permanently changed.

A young girl we recently hired at the Hour of Power belongs to the Roman Catholic Church and receives a Roman Catholic publication called the Liguorian. She thought we would be interested in an article in the Liguorian written by Pete Dunham.

Pete Dunham is still serving his term in Soledad Prison where he has been for over ten years. The article is entitled, "I Was Imprisoned and You Wrote Me":

"The guard stopped by my cell in Soledad Prison several weeks ago and delivered a letter from Dr. Robert Schuller, pastor of the Garden Grove Community Church, in Garden Grove, California. Reverend Schuller's Hour of Power television ministry is one of the most widely viewed television religious services in the world. Excitedly I opened the letter and read its contents twice. It assured me that I was not alone, that I was loved by Christ and by Reverend Schuller's congregation, and that I was being remembered in prayer each week. The letter climaxed several months of internal debate which resulted in my conversion to Christianity.

"I entered prison for a narcotics offense as a young

hoodlum, full of ideas of macho imagery and false allegiances. My peers, like myself, were immature, self-centered and trouble-oriented. We scoffed at religion, and those among our number who attended religious services widely held the belief that churchgoers were weak, homosexuals and informers. No so-called regular would ever go to church."

Then he tells of receiving a letter from a beautiful Roman Catholic sister which touched him deeply and of how he entered into a correspondence with our Hour of Power ministry. He said, "It was not until I was finally able to purchase a small portable television for my cell a few months ago that I unconsciously found myself listening—half in awe, half in disbelief—to the messages that Dr. Schuller was telecasting and watching the faces of the people sitting there in the pews and in the garden.

"Dr. Schuller spoke of love, happiness and success, and the people seemed to have it. These were the three things most lacking in my life. Slowly I became aware that I was silently joining them in prayer and even in song in my cell. I started asking God for forgiveness and help and asked His blessings on my parents and loved ones. I was praying, asking for direction and strength, when suddenly I became a new person, a Christian, in prison.

"Some day I hope to meet Reverend Schuller and shake hands with him."

All this because of a letter that said, "I care."

Alter your altar and everything changes.

I invite you now, whoever you are, to check your buttons, check your value system, check your philosophy, check your religion or your lack of it. God has a plan for you.

"For I know the plans I have for you," says the Lord. "They are plans for good and not for evil, to give you a future and a hope" (Jeremiah 29:11).

# *Discover*
# *Health And*
# *Happiness*

# 1

## *Your Deepest Need—*
## *Feed It*

I ask you this question: *"What is your deepest need?"*

Of course, you need air to breathe, water to drink, food to eat, for without these three needs being met, your body would die.

I admit, however, there is a deeper need than any of these. For what good is it if you have a living body when you don't have a thriving, living, enthusiastic, joy-filled, optimistic, strong spirit?

What you need more than air, or water, or food is Spirit that can put real power and life within you.

What is your deepest need? I'll give you some clues. You need it when you face your dreams. You need it when you are confronted with opportunity. You need it when you have to make a big decision. You also need it when you face your toughest problem.

You need it when you are a young person. You need it when you are getting married. You need it when you get old. You need it when you are ready to breathe your last breath. It will be the last need you will have in life. When the time and the moment comes that you do not need another swallow of water, or another bite of food, or another breath of air, *you will still need this!*

What need am I talking about? Your deepest need summed up in one word is HOPE! Without hope you are finished! With hope you have everything! St. Paul, in Romans 12:12, speaks of "Rejoicing in hope." The Psalmist says, "Hope thou in God for I shall yet trust him" (see Psalm 42:5).

This age will be known not only as the age where

man went to the moon, it will also be known as the tranquilizing age, and as the age when people had problems with drug addiction, alcoholism, gross immorality and pornography. Why? Because this is an age without hope. Take away hope and men become desperate. They will seek an escape from the reality of life; and they seek to escape either in drunkenness, or pills, or dope, or promiscuity. These are all ways of "copping out" on life—a form of quitting!

I read the story of a little boy's first day in kindergarten. When his mother asked how he liked school, he answered, "I quit." She said, "What do you mean? One day in school and you quit?" He said, "I can't read, I can't write and the teacher won't let me talk. So why go back?"

"I quit." *Without hope you become a quitter.*

Did you hear about the father who was trying to encourage his teenage son? He was having trouble in high school and was threatening to drop out. "Dad," he said, "I am going to quit." His dad said, "Son, the people who are remembered in life are the people who never quit. Remember Fulton? He didn't quit! Eli Whitney? He didn't quit! Thomas Jefferson? Thomas Edison? They didn't quit!" The boy agreed, nodding. His father went on, "Isadore McCringle?" The boy said, "Who is Isadore McCringle, Dad?" The father said, "See, you don't remember him! He quit!"

I was in New York recently and picked up a poster which I sent to my son, who is a freshman in college. He is doing very well, but he is struggling with a course in Russian history. So I sent him this large poster. It is a picture of a boy, probably eighteen years of age, in his football uniform. He is sitting on a bench and has thrown his helmet down. His face is covered with mud, his hair disheveled, and his hands are folded dejectedly across his chest. The caption reads, "I quit." Down on the bottom of the poster is a little picture of a black hill; on it is a very tiny cross, and next to it these words, "I didn't."

If you have hope, you will never quit! No matter what happens!

Charles Beard, a great American historian, came to the end of his career and was asked what great lessons he had learned from history. He announced, "I have learned four. First, whom the gods would destroy they first make mad with power. Second, the mills of God grind slowly, yet they grind exceedingly fine. Third, the bee fertilizes the flower it robs. Fourth, when it is dark enough you will be able to see the stars."

I will never forget one of the most moving moments in my life. The first of my five children was leaving home. Her name is Sheila. I was taking her to the airport to fly East where she was going to enroll in college. I knew that when she left for college we were really losing our first child from the home. It was the beginning of the break-up of the form that the family had enjoyed for many years. Mrs. Schuller decided to stay at home and said, "Bob, you just drive Sheila to the airport alone." She kissed Sheila at the door and the two of us walked to the car. I put her bags in the trunk and we rode silently down the freeway.

After a long period of silence, I finally said, "Sheila, what are you thinking about?" She answered, "Oh, I was just thinking, Dad, about some words you had in your sermon some time back." I replied, "Oh, that's interesting. What words are they?" She quoted them perfectly as she looked at me with misty eyes and a smile on her face . . . "Grieve not for me, who am about to start a new adventure. Eager I stand, and ready to depart, me and my reckless pioneering heart!"

Hope . . . you need it at the beginning, in the middle, and at the end of life.

Recently I was on a cruise with the Chapman College Summer School. We had in our student body a woman we all affectionately called Grandma Finley. She was eighty-four years of age. When we docked in New

Zealand, the people were so impressed to learn that we had an 84-year-old student on board that they sent a newspaper reporter to interview her. The reporter asked her, "Have you cruised many times?" (Of course. She does nothing but travel around the world! She is one of the world's greatest travelers. She has been in Russia, I think she said, six times!) Then the reporter asked, "Well, Grandma Finley, I suppose this is your last cruise?" She was shocked! "Oh no," she replied emphatically, "it can't be . . . because I belong to CMT club!" "The CMT club? What is the CMT club?" the reporter asked. She snapped back, "Can't Miss a Thing!"

You need hope when you are young, you need hope when you are old. *It is the one thing every human being needs.*

What happens when you have hope? Dreams begin to take root instead of vanishing into thin air! When you don't have hope, a dream fades away! It never becomes a concrete reality. Without hope, decisions go unmade, opportunities pass, somebody else grabs them and you come in a "Johnny-come-lately" second.

Without hope, problems overpower, stop, block, stagger, stumble and trip you! That is what happens without hope. Show me a person who has hope and I'll see a person in whom dreams take root where opportunities are grasped, and problems are solved chip by chip, splinter by splinter, stone by stone, until the obstacle is gone! All this happens through the mysterious power we call *hope*.

# 2

## Find Hope,
## And Discover Life!

What is hope? What is this phenomenal spirit? I use that word scientifically because of a psychiatrist who lectured for thirty-five minutes at the Madrid Psychiatric Congress several years ago. I remember that he spoke on one single theme!

*"Hope!* What is it?" he said. The thousands of psychiatrists who were sitting there in the auditorium leaned forward, as I did, for he was about to focus, to analyze, and to put the psychiatric microscope upon this phenomenal spirit called hope. He paused, and repeated the question, "What is it? I don't know! Nobody knows! All we know is that we have all had patients who came to us week after week, month after month, and they sat there with their depressed, discouraged, despondent faces, skin hanging almost grey in color, like an old cloth hanging over dead bones, and their eyes flat, dull, and devoid of sparkle. Week after week they came back to us—listless, lethargic, dejectedly sitting down as lifeless as a sack of potatoes, without form, structure, energy or life. Then, as we talked to them, and listened to them, we suddenly saw a mysterious spark glitter in their eyes, grey skin became pink, those flat eyes became round, cheeks that were sunken began to blossom. All we can say is, *hope was born!* But what is it? Where does it come from? We do not know."

I sat there in that seat and said to myself, "I know! You call it *hope*—I call it *God!* It is the very Spirit of God Himself! That's what *hope* is!" Some people say, "Where there is life, there is hope." I turn it around and

192

say, "Where there is hope, there is Life. Where there's Hope—there's God!"

While visiting New Zealand, somebody said to me, "Dr. Schuller, you must meet Jim Franklin, Jr. He is a young 24-year-old guy who is right on your wave length. He is a great possibility thinker." So when our ship docked in port there was a call waiting for me from him. I met him. What a fantastic guy!

He took me to the headquarters of a broadcasting station. As we walked around he introduced me to the key men. He said, "Dr. Schuller, there is a great story here. A story of hope, faith, and belief! A story that proves that with possibility thinking anything can be done." Then he unfolded this story:

Several years ago, a few young fellows decided it would be a great thing if New Zealand had a private radio station that could broadcast the news of a positive, happy religion. But, of course, New Zealand is a socialistic state and all the broadcasting facilities are owned by the state. No private, independent radio stations were permitted by law. So these young guys got together and decided they would simply change the law! Older experts told them that this was impossible! "Because this is a socialistic state you'll never do it!" they said. By now their number had increased to twenty-four young men. Their average age was twenty-four years. They were totally convinced that New Zealand would be a better nation if it had some private commercial radio stations.

So they decided to form a corporation, hire a lawyer and figure out how they might change the law! The first thing the lawyer said to them was, "Boys" (I think he called them kids), "it is impossible! You know it is impossible!" They said, "Okay, get out. We will hire a smarter lawyer." He hedged nervously. "Now wait. Just a minute," he said. They retorted, "We are paying you to find a legal loophole!" He answered, "But there are no legal loopholes." To which they replied, *"We are hiring you to figure out how you can create a legal loophole!* Now, remember, our average age is twenty-four; we want to see it done before we retire! That gives you forty years! Can you do it in forty years?" Stunned, he left.

Two weeks later he called the boys and said, "Hey, kids, I found a loophole." (It is an astonishing thing, but when hope is born, people begin to spot solutions where before they never thought even a chance existed!) The lawyer reported enthusiastically. "If you can put a radio broadcasting station on a ship, and if you could put the ship to sea, anchor twelve miles off the coast, then you could transmit to the coast of New Zealand!" Continuing, he explained, "It would be a pirate operation, but it would be legal from an international standpoint." They replied, "Great!"

So they called another meeting. "Now, all we need is a boat, and the transmitting equipment to go on it." Well, they prayed about it until one of the boys said, "I happen to know somebody who owns several ships and I know he is a very devoted Christian man. I think that he might let us use one of his ships."

They called him immediately. The shipowner was quick to answer, "Yes," he said, "I do have this ship; it is anchored right here in Auckland, New Zealand. For your cause, I would let you use it! The only thing is, I must tell you that you can't take the ship out of port without a permit from the Minister of Maritime Activities! (That's a government official.) Now, what you boys don't know is that the Minister of Maritime Activities is also the Minister of Communications! Which means that if he finds out you want to take this ship out to sea to put a pirate radio station on the air—well, forget it! I will not allow my ship to be sailing under any deceit or duplicity!"

Well, that ended that! Or did it!

The boys got together and some possibility thinker made a suggestion. "Let's not quit," he said. "When it is time to quit, do you know what time it is! It's time to call a prayer meeting!" So they started praying again. As they were praying, one of the boys interrupted, "I've got an idea! Let's go talk to the Minister of Maritime Activities and tell him we want this ship to sail."

It was a crazy idea, but they decided to talk to him. "What do you want to use this ship for?" he asked. They said, "Well, sir, we cannot be dishonest. We feel that New Zealand, great though it is with all of its radio stations that you control so marvelously, sir, could be enriched if there could be one private commercial station. It would add a little spice to the country we think."

He frowned as he looked at them, and his response shocked them. He said, "Do you know what? I think so, too! Secretly, that is, for I can't say too much as a government official. But I'll tell you what I will do. If you want to send that ship out and broadcast twelve miles off the coast, I won't stop that ship from going out! If after two years of broadcasting you do such a good job that the citizens of our country say they want this station to broadcast legally, and if there is grass roots pressure to legitimize the operation, I will cooperate."

The boys were jubilant! They collected the equipment and the ship sailed. Then they started broadcasting to the island. After twenty-four months, the Minister of Communications had received tens of thousands of letters, so many that when they applied for the permit, it was granted! And they established, legally, on the mainland what is today the first independent free enterprise, privately owned commercial radio broadcasting station in New Zealand!

Think of it! A group of fellows in their twenties, with hope in their hearts, changed the law of the land! Today there are hundreds of thousands of people who are getting enthusiastic messages about Jesus Christ over this private radio station. Anything is possible when there is hope!

Hope! . . . that mysterious force that makes dreams take root! What do you call that power? I call it God! Get hope and you have everything!

How do you get it? Where does it come from? How do you get this kind of spirit when you need it desper-

ately? I will tell you this . . . no counselor can ultimately give it to you! No minister can finally give it to
you! I don't know a psychiatrist or psychologist who
can give it to you. Any minister, any counselor, any the-
ologian, any religious leader, any psychologist or any
psychiatrist who says, "I did it," may have removed an
emotional block; that's possible. But where did that
spirit come from? *God did it!* How do you get this
spirit? I know only one way . . . that is by drawing
close to God!

Dr. Peale tells an amazing story about a time he was
scheduled to speak at a large convention. The appointment had been made a year and a half in advance.
Loads of money had been spent to prepare for his coming. "The time arrived," he says, "and I flew into town.
I arrived in the afternoon. The speech was to be given
that night. They told me that five thousand people were
coming to hear me. Soon thereafter, laryngitis began to
set in on my vocal cords. My voice began to leave and I
really became concerned.

"I called the doctor and said, 'Doctor, can you spray
my vocal cords?' He came over to the hotel, checked
me over and said, 'Yes, I can spray them if you want
me to.' I said, 'I think you had better.' So he sprayed
my vocal cords. When he finished the treatment, I said,
'Can't you give me some pills?' The doctor said, 'Well, I
can give you some if you want some.' So he gave me
some pills.

"Then the doctor sat down on the chair, looked at me
and said, 'Dr. Peale, I have sprayed your throat, I've
given you some pills, but now I would like to give you
the treatment that can really heal you.' I said, 'Why did
you wait so long? What is it?' 'Because,' the doctor said,
'I didn't think I would have to give it to *you!*' I'm a
positive thinker, so I said, 'Give it to me! I'll take it!'
The doctor said, 'It is called the golden key.' 'The
golden key?' I asked. 'What is that?' Smiling, the doctor
explained, 'The golden key is this: *Focus your thoughts
on God; don't focus them on your problem.* You have
been focusing your thoughts on your problem! That

tightens up your nervous system so the blood doesn't flow harmoniously. As a result, you experience sickness. Stop focusing on the problem, and start focusing on God.' I focused on God. When I walked to the platform to speak that night, I testify that my voice was never stronger than it was that night."

The golden key—here's how to find hope! Don't focus on your need. Don't focus on your lack. Don't focus on your problem. Focus on God. *Where does hope come from*? Hope comes from the Silence! Do you remember in the Bible that despairing creature called Elijah? There came a time when he was so depressed he wanted to die. But he was too much of a godly man to commit suicide, so he simply prayed, "God, take my soul." But he didn't die.

Suddenly he heard the wind blow. The wind turned over rocks that tumbled in dust down the hillside, smashing themselves in the valleys below. The wind twisted the branches, tearing them bleeding from the trees and casting them in a pile of leaves on the ground. He said, "Ah, God is in the wind." But God said, "I am not in the wind."

Then he felt the earth begin to move and he said, "God is in the earthquake." But God said, "I am not in the earthquake."

The Bible goes on, "Suddenly there was a still small voice! God came to him out of the Silence!"

In the musical, "1776," George Washington asked these questions: Is anybody there: Is anybody listening? Does anybody care? The answer is: There is Some One there! There is Some One listening! There is Some One who cares! He wants to touch you now!

That's what I've been doing all my life—following the fellow who follows a dream . . . His name is Jesus Christ. He is at the innermost core of my heart. There is that still, silent, sacred corner where He keeps my hope throbbing and vibrant!

Ask Christ to come into your life and *hope* will be born again deep down in your heart!

There is Some One there!
   There is Some One listening!
There is Some One who cares!
   His name is God.
He wants to touch you now!

# 3

## *How To Handle Your Negative Emotions*

Another step in making health and happiness yours is to learn this truth: *There are positive emotions and negative emotions.* Water can power a generator and turn out electricity, or it can overflow the river banks, flood homes and destroy life. In the same way, emotions can be destructive or constructive—positive or negative.

Look at Jesus Christ. Part of the secret of His greatness was that the positive emotions dominated Him:

Courage instead of fear,
Hope instead of despair
Confidence instead of cynicism,
Love instead of hate,
Belief instead of doubt.

Show me a person who is dominated by the positive emotions, and nine times out of ten I will show you a person in whose heart Jesus Christ is living, in a very real and in a very vital way.

I would like you to do something—an assignment. Take a piece of paper and on the top of one side write the word, *Positive.* On the other side write the word, *Negative.* Try to analyze your own feelings. List all the positive feelings you have, then make a list of the negative feelings. Do this until you have described all the feelings you can think of about yourself.

Now, for every positive emotion, there is also a negative emotion. For instance, under

> The negative emotions you would write despair—the opposite would be hope.
>
> The negative emotion would be fear—the positive would be courage.
>
> The negative emotion would be lethargy—the positive emotion would be ambition.
>
> The negative emotion would be resignation and defeat—the positive emotion would be determination.
>
> The negative emotion would be hate—the positive would be love.
>
> The negative emotion would be doubt—the positive emotion would be faith.
>
> The negative emotion would be cynicism—the positive emotion would be optimism.
>
> The negative emotion would be worry—the positive emotion would be trust.
>
> The negative emotion would be suspicion—the positive emotion would be belief.
>
> The negative emotion would be self-hate—the positive emotion would be self-confidence.
>
> The negative emotion would be inferiority feelings—the positive emotion would be the certainty that "I can do it, and I am as good as any other person; after all, God made me, too."

Now, make your own list, because no two people are alike. When you have the list drawn, then circle the feelings that dominate you. If you circle more negative emotions than positive emotions, then you know you have an emotional problem. But, you will also know what your problem is! You will know that you are dominated by these negative emotions. If you know what your problem is, you may not have to go to a psychiatrist. Perhaps all you may need to do is replace the negative emotions with their positive counterparts.

Now, how can you control the negative emotions? I am going to offer you seven suggestions that I know will work for you if you will work with them.

*Principle No. 1*—Verbalize them away.

A word of warning is in order. First: Never verbalize a negative emotion *out loud, alone.* That is very important! In other words, if you feel you are no good, if you feel you are not pretty, if you feel you have blown it, if you feel you are a failure, if you feel your life is a wash-out, you must never, *never verbalize such a negative emotion alone.* If you are driving your car, or if you are lying in your bed, or if you are walking on a sidewalk— don't ever verbalize a negative emotion alone because your conscious mind will believe it and you will just be plummeted down to defeat and despair.

A second word of caution: *Never verbalize a negative emotion out loud to another negative-thinking person* because he will agree with you! He will say, "Yeah, you sure blew it, didn't you!" And that will really defeat you!

A third note of caution: *Never verbalize a negative emotion in an exclamatory sentence!* How then do you verbalize a negative emotion?

Here's how: *By putting it in the form of a question, and then addressing it to a positive-thinking person.*

For instance: If you think your marriage is washed up, you don't say out loud, as you are driving to work, "My marriage is washed up, I'm finished." As soon as you say that, you are! Nor do you stop at the bar on the way home and say to the bartender, "You know, I think my marriage is washed up." He will say, "I think you are right. Have another beer." What do you do? You go to a pastor, or to a counsellor, or to some other positive-thinking Christian.

Now you don't say to your pastor, "Pastor, my marriage is washed up." What you do is to ask a question: "Is there any hope for saving my marriage? Is it possible there might be some effective way we can rebuild love after what has happened?" Principle No. 1 comes into play at this point: You verbalize a negative emotion by putting it in the form of a question, and you address that question to a possibility-thinking, positive, emotion-charged person. *That is how to verbalize it!* You will be surprised how many of your bad feelings can be discharged this way.

*Principle No. 2*—Exercise them away.

If you can't talk them out, walk them out. Walk a mile . . . walk two! My wife said, "You can tell the people that when I get negative emotions I wash and polish dishes and silverware." We have a beautiful marriage because I don't convey my negative emotions to my wife, nor does she to me. She polishes the silverware; I weed the lawn!

A psychiatrist advised a woman who was suffering from arthritis to physically work the negative emotions out of her organism. He knew that her arthritis was caused by deep-seated hostility, resentments, jealousies and hate. So he told her to go out and buy a bag of marbles and a hammer. He instructed her to put those marbles on the cement sidewalk and smash the marbles with the hammer. It cured her!

*Principle No. 3*—Analyze them away.

How do you analyze your emotions away? First of all, by reminding yourself that a negative emotion is always an exaggeration.

A negative emotion is seldom completely reliable. In retrospect, you can almost always look back and say that the negative emotions were the ones that deceived you the most.

Now, analyze and recognize that negative emotions are seeds. Remember, if you plant a negative seed you can expect to raise negative fruit. Express the negative emotion and you can expect negative results. If you plant thistles, don't expect to harvest grapes.

Ask yourself, "How important will this problem appear to me one year from now? Two years from now? Three years, four years, ten years from now?"

A young man was in to see me some time ago. He was all upset. He was 32 years of age, a brilliant college graduate, and one of the sharpest men in his company. He was sure he was going to fill the slot of the vice-presidency, when, lo and behold, the board moved in a man who was 55 years old. He said to me with bitter disappointment, "The guy is an old duffer! I was really counting on that promotion!" His lament touched me. I said, "Well, take the long look. How important is this ten years from now?" Suddenly his mouth dropped open. "Oh, ten years from now," he said, thoughtfully, "he will have to retire! That's right! He won't have this job long! And in ten years I will only be 42!"

Analyze your negative feelings. You will be amazed to find how many negative emotions can be exercised away, verbalized away, or analyzed away.

*Principle No. 4*—Paralyze them away.

The beautiful thing about Jesus Christ is that He came to heal our negative emotions. For every negative emotion, Jesus Christ gives a positive emotion, and a positive emotion will neutralize or paralyze a negative emotion. In other words, you can't be fearful and courageous at the same time. You can't be full of guilt and full of forgiveness at the same time. You can't be full of anger and full of love at the same time. It is an impossibility.

So, for every negative emotion Jesus Christ came to offer a positive, curative counterpart! Faith instead of doubt, hope in place of despair, love in place of hate, salvation in place of sin, forgiveness in place of guilt.

We know that the taproot of all negative emotion is, as the Bible calls it, sin. What is that? Sin is being separated from God. Sin is doing things you should not do and feeling guilty because of it. But salvation paralyzes the negative emotions caused by sin.

*Principle No. 5*—Hypnotize them away, with positive affirmations.

Now, don't let this word "hypnotize" frighten you. Let me give you a definition of hypnosis. Hypnosis is nothing more than the free surrender of the conscious will to the domination of a dynamic thought. In this definition, every one of us is hypnotized every time that we freely choose to submit our conscious mind to the domination of a dynamic thought. Dynamic thoughts can be either positive or negative. Fear is a negative dynamic thought, and it can dominate you. Faith is a positive dynamic thought, and it can dominate you. You are either dominated or hypnotized by a positive or a negative thought, and it happens constantly. You say, "I am going to drive down the Santa Ana Freeway to Los Angeles." That is a thought. When you surrender your conscious will to that thought, you have hypnotized yourself to action. To be hypnotized doesn't mean that your eyes are closed; it doesn't mean that you are in a trance.

I remember when my wife had her last two babies through hypnosis. It was totally painless childbirth. She was wide awake and enjoying every minute of it! And the nurses in the delivery room kept asking her: "Shall we give you a shot? It must be hurting." "No," she said, "I am feeling sensations and contractions of the body, but it does not hurt; there is no pain!" Hypnosis is not being in a trance, it is being dominated by a concept or an idea.

When St. Paul said, "I can do all things through Christ who strengthens me," he was hypnotizing himself with a positive affirmation. He decided that he was going to surrender his will to the affirmation, and *that is faith!*

So, there are many people who call themselves Christians; they say they have been born again; they can recite the Bible from memory; they can really give you a doctrinal lecture! But they are despairing, miserable, negative, faultfinding, critical people. Why? Because they have never learned the secret of a dynamic faith.

Faith is surrendering yourself to the positive ideas that come from Jesus Christ until you are hypnotized to positive feeling and action!

*Principle No. 6*—Sterilize away your negative emotions.

Take the poison out of the passion. I mean, very simply, take the sin out of the negative emotion. You can do that with this one question—ask yourself, "Am I being selfish about this?" You will be surprised to find how many negative feelings will be settled then and there. You don't want to be a selfish person. So you will drop your bad feelings!

Sterilize your negative emotions. Ask Jesus Christ to come into your heart. Say to Him, "Jesus Christ, come in. Save me from my selfishness and sin. Save me now from my negative emotions, Jesus Christ! Save me from my selfishness! Amen."

*Principle No. 7*—If you can't exercise them, or verbalize them, or analyze them, or paralyze them, or hypnotize them, or sterilize them away—then try this: Fertilize the positive emotions!

We had trouble with dandelions in our back lawn in Santa Ana until we planted dichondra, and the dichondra choked out the dandelions! Fill your life with a dynamic, positive faith and fear goes. If fear goes, jealousy will go, resentment will go, and hate will go. A positive faith will do more than anything else to straighten out your emotions.

The important thing is, do you really have a dynamic positive faith? Faith will wipe out fear!

When I traveled to the Soviet Union recently, I was cautioned not to identify myself as a priest, or a pastor, or a religious leader but as a professor which incidentally, I could do in good conscience. So I went as a professor. One of the major objectives of our mission to Russia was to meet with underground churchmen in Lvov, a city in the western part of the Ukraine. "My instructions are," I reminded myself, "to maintain a low profile as I travel through the country. I am not to fear for my own safety, but I have to realize that if I am followed, I may lead the KGB people to the secret underground churchmen, and these Christians would find themselves in prison."

My instructions also included the schedule I was to follow and the details of the rendezvous. On Tuesday I was to take the plane from Leningrad to Kiev, where I would make a thirty-five minute transfer to Lvov, arriving there Tuesday evening. I was to sleep there Tuesday night and in the morning, between nine and ten o'clock, I was to wait in the hotel lobby to be met there by a leader of the underground church.

I was further instructed that this man was to approach me and say, "Do you know where Garden Grove, California, is?" I was to answer, "Yes." The man would then turn and walk out of the hotel lobby, and I would then follow him at a safe distance for a few blocks, until it seemed safe for us to rendezvous. We would then go to a secret underground church meeting.

Now, on Tuesday at two o'clock in the afternoon, the day before I was to make my contact in Lvov, I was exposed in a Leningrad museum. It was the Museum of Atheism. I was shocked to see a picture of myself in the pulpit of our church. The guide soon identified me. What really shook me was that my plane was scheduled to leave for Kiev within two hours.

The question began to burn in my mind: *"What do I do about tomorrow morning's rendezvous? Do I keep it, or don't I?* If I don't keep it, I may miss a great spiritual experience. I may miss the opportunity to inspire the church that will be meeting in secret. But if I keep this appointment, will I be followed? Will I endanger the lives of the secret believers?" The questions kept me worried. It was one of the most anxious moments of my life. *Not because of what would happen to me, but because of what could happen to innocent believers.*

At four o'clock we boarded our plane in Leningrad and flew to Kiev. An Intourist guide was waiting to receive us and to assist us in transferring to another plane which was to leave for Lvov in thirty-five minutes. The Intourist guide said, "Your plane leaves from another airport." He promptly put us in a cab, said something to the driver, and sent us off.

My companion, Mr. Eichenberger, and I sat in the back, fully expecting to be driven to the next building. Instead, the cab headed out into the country! We passed through a grove of trees, and away from the airport! Since we had only thirty-five minutes between planes, I became uneasy. I said to Mr. Eichenberger, "I don't think we are headed for another airport. Perhaps we are being called in for interrogation." So we agreed on the answers we would give to their questions, if they interviewed us separately. I began to think of all the things that I had said to the guides during my stay in their country, things that I would not have said if I had known I would be exposed as a minister.

Suddenly we saw the skyscrapers of a city ahead of us. By now thirty minutes had passed! We knew we were not going to make a thirty-five-minute plane transfer! The ride continued until it became pitch dark and our headlights pierced the darkness. At this point we approached an entrance to grounds that looked very formal. On either side of the road we saw the big red star which now we recognized to be the symbol of the Red Army. We therefore expected to be ushered into the headquarters of the Red Army. To our surprise, we discovered it to be an army airport.

Our cab driver stopped in front of a building and we were ordered upstairs and into a room. The door closed behind us. We were ordered to sit down. Military people paced up and down, chattering incessantly in Russian. Forty minutes passed. An hour passed. Two hours passed! Unable to hold back any longer, I spoke out, "We have to get to Lvov tonight!" I was insistent. No one understood me, so I drew a picture of a litle train, with an arrow pointing from Kiev to Lvov. (It is amazing what you can do with pictures!) "Nyet, nyet," they said, meaning "No, no."

Now, it was nearly midnight, and they finally realized

how upset we were. (At that moment we discovered that in Russia, they don't want to get people upset, so they'll do anything to keep up a good front!) So, in order to get us to calm down they found an English-speaking person who said, "You will not go to Lvov tonight. There is an unexpected thunderstorm. You can hear it thunder now! There are no planes leaving. You will not go to Lvov tonight. We will put you in a hotel. Tomorrow morning we will put you on the first plane to Lvov. You will get to Lvov at 11:30 a.m. tomorrow!" We went to the hotel and the next morning we boarded our plane. We arrived in Lvov, and were at our hotel at 11:45, about forty-five minutes past the hour of our rendezvous! It was now too late to meet anyone!

Now, the interesting thing is that I have flown over a half million miles in the past twenty-one years, and in my twenty-one years of flying around this world, only once have I ever missed a flight where bad weather had caused the plane to be grounded! I have flown in tough weather in Alaska, I have flown through storms in Korea, and only twice have I not made a flight because the plane was grounded due to bad weather! That happened on that Tuesday in Russia!

*God kept the plane down to keep us from rendezvousing the next morning with the underground churchmen!* For I did not know until I got back to the hotel that I would be spied on by the KGB. One of their agents was on the outside of the front door, another was on the outside of the side door, and still another was posted right outside the door to our room! This last one happened to be a woman. She logged us in when we went into the room and she logged us out when we went out. We were under constant surveillance, and we would certainly have led the underground church people to a prison cell!

I tell you, I believe in God! He does guide! He does lead! I want to encourage you to give your soul that kind of positive faith. Through faith, Jesus Christ will fill your heart so full of positive emotions, that all negative emotions will simply be choked out!

There is a positive emotion to replace every negative emotion. When a negative emotion rises up within, you can sing the praises of God knowing He is planning something beautiful. You can cling to the promises of God, for He is faithful. And you can fertilize all the positive emotions God is stirring up within you.

# Discover Courage
## To Face
## Your Future

# 1

## Dare To Step
## Into Tomorrow

If I could give you one quality today by the grace and power of God it would be courage—the courage to take the step that can change your life! You can become a new you if you will dare to step into the tomorrow that God has planned for you!

I have to admit that the inspiration for my title came from a letter that I received from my good friend, Frank Sinatra. He sent me a beautiful long and personal letter and I'd like to share a few lines with you. He writes, "Dr. Schuller, your television messages are medicine to my mind. Somehow, every time I listen to your messages, I have the courage to step into tomorrow!" Those are powerful words! *You too can have the courage to step into tomorrow!*

We had a wonderful Christmas this past year except for one little problem. It rained. We have a cozy little mountain cottage up in Big Bear, California. My son and I practically built it with our own hands, eleven years ago. Every winter we spend some time up there, enjoying the peace and quiet and the beautiful snow. But this Christmas we went up to our cabin and it was raining! There was no snow, just rain and mud slides. What a disappointment to everybody! And then, to top it off, our roof leaked! Water was dripping on my head as I tried to put pails under all the leaks.

Before long I became a little bit irritated and started preaching a sermon to the cabin. "This is disgusting!" I exclaimed. "Here I am with water dripping on my head and I can't even go outside because there it's pouring down rain! Don't you know who I am?" I asked, ignor-

ing the stares of my family. I went on, "Remember when we first met? I was only a carpenter but now I am a preacher! And this cannot go on. I'm not going to come back here and spend another three days during the Christmas season and let you douse me with water." That little outburst really helped me for it relieved all the tension that was stored up inside!

When we got all the pails situated, I set about trying to find something for my two youngest girls to do. And I did something that I have never done before in my entire life. I took my children downtown to the only place where there was any action—THE ARCADE! What an experience! Lights were flashing and bells were ringing everywhere! I had never been in such a confusing place in my life. It was a mass of human beings, body to body, feeding quarters and nickels and dimes into machines.

"Girls!" I shouted, "We came to the mountains for peace and tranquility! This is too much! Let's get out of here!" But just as I turned to leave the Arcade I spotted a tall blond haired young man standing on the opposite side of the room. He was very tall and appeared to be staring at me. I could see him pressing

through the crowd, trying to get to me before I took off out the door. Suspecting that maybe he was a friend that had seen me on television I decided to wait until he reached me. He kept coming through the crowd as fast as he could until he was only five feet away from me.

The young man stared at me with intensity. I smiled and extended my hand. "Are you Reverend Schuller?" he asked as he warmly shook my hand. "Yes," I answered. "You're neat," he exclaimed. "Well, thank you," I said. Then he continued. "I watch you on television every Sunday. You've really changed my life!"

He was excited as he spoke to me. During the entire conversation we were standing in the middle of the Arcade amidst the crowds and the noise, but neither of us seemed to notice.

"You have a mountain cabin up here, don't you?" he continued. "Why, yes," I replied. "And somebody broke in a couple of years ago and stole your television set, stereo and your son's skis, right?" Now I was really confused. "How did you know?" I queried. "I'm the one who did it," he explained. "And I really feel bad about it. I was only 17 and I was a bad kid. But they caught us and you know all about that." "Yes," I replied, "I was asked to go to court and testify but I was out of town so the judge handled it without my coming up here." "I'm really sorry, Dr. Schuller, but you did get all your things back undamaged, right?" he asked. "Yes, I went down to the police station to identify the stolen goods," I assured him.

Before my young friend left I had to ask him, "How did you get into my cabin?" "Oh," he said, "it was easy. I climbed up the outside to the sliding glass door on the second level. Somebody had left it open. By the way," he added, "after the court proceeding somebody came up to me and said, 'Do you know whose cabin you ripped off?' And I said, 'No.' And my friend said, 'You broke into Dr. Schuller's place!' 'Oh, yeah?' I exclaimed. 'Who's he?' 'He's the minister at the Garden Grove Community Church. He's on television every Sunday!' he explained. And that's when I started watching you on television!"

"Are you a Christian?" I asked. "I don't know, but I sure want to be. How do I become a Christian?" he responded. "Well," I said, "just exactly the way you are going about it. You go up to somebody who is a Christian and ask them! It begins by living your life with Jesus Christ. You need to say: Dear Jesus Christ, I know I have sinned. You know that too. I need forgiveness. I need salvation. I need to be a more beautiful person. And I want you to come into my heart and mind and change me. I love you and I want to be like you."

"Would you like to offer that kind of a prayer?" I asked my young friend. "Sure," he enthusiastically replied. "We can do that right here and now if you don't mind," I said. "No, I don't mind," he enthused. And right there in the middle of the Arcade on Main Street in Big Bear, California, I offered a prayer and he repeated after me. Then we gave each other a hug.

"Do you have any Christian friends?" I asked. "Well," he said, "the kid that was with me when I broke into your cabin just recently found Jesus and he's going to a Bible group this week." "Good," I enthusiastically encouraged. "Go with him! And I'd like to send you some books for a daily, mental and spiritual treat, okay?"

I don't believe I've ever met a young man that had more courage than he did! It's unbelievable how human beings change! You can be a new you! Old or new, it's up to you! There's a great new you waiting to come through if you will take the right steps! You can have the courage to make the decision! God Almighty believes in you! When somebody believes in you and tells you they believe in you, before you know it, you begin to believe in yourself. The confidence that somebody else has in you becomes a self-fulfilling expectation that is placed on the subconscious level of your mind until your new expectation of yourself becomes literally a self-fulfilling prediction!

# 2

## *The Past Can Be Changed*

A very good friend of mine stood in this pulpit one Sunday morning several years ago and delivered one of the most inspiring messages I have ever heard. Bill Sands is in heaven today but when he stood before this congregation—what a message he shared! I remember when, in the course of his message he put his finger on his nose and it totally flattened out. There was no cartilage left in Bill's nose because it had been beaten out by convicts in San Quentin prison. His nose had been flattened by lead pipes and by the fists of tough guards.

It was on the second of July in 1941 that Bill Sands stood in the courtroom and heard the judge pronounce his sentence: Not less than one year nor more than life in San Quentin! Months later, the word, INCORRIGIBLE was stamped on his file. Think of that word. What a negative, ghastly, destructive label! *INCORRIGIBLE!* He was not eligible for parole. He would never get out of prison! But then something happened. Clinton Duffy was appointed warden of San Quentin and soon after arrival, he paid Bill a visit. "Bill," Duffy said, in a grave but courteous tone. "How would you like these walls to melt like butter? Or how would you like the iron bars to turn into water so you could just walk out?" Bill looked up at Duffy and sarcastically said, "Duffy, who are you kidding? I know what is on my record. It says in bold red letters: *INCORRIGIBLE—* not eligible for parole." "Bill," Warden Duffy exclaimed, "that's true, but let me tell you something else. I believe in you! I believe you can become a new you!

215

God can help you change." That was the beginning of a new life for Bill Sands!

*There is somebody who believes in you and that somebody is Jesus Christ!* It takes courage to step into that new life and become a Christian. You'll be stepping into a new tomorrow; a different culture; a different life-style; a different collection of friends. A lot of things will change! That's why it takes courage! And if there is one thing Jesus Christ wants to give you today, it is courage! Courage to step into tomorrow!

In 1921, Lewis Lawes became the warden at Sing Sing Prison. No prison was tougher than Sing Sing during that time. But when Warden Lawes retired 20 some years later, that prison had become a humanitarian institution. It was a model for other prisons to follow. Those who studied the system said credit for the change belonged to Lewis Lawes. But when Warden Lawes was asked about the transformation, this is what he said: "I owe it all to my wonderful wife, Catherine, who is buried outside the prison walls."

Catherine Lawes was a young mother with three small children when her husband became the warden at Sing Sing Prison. Everybody warned her from the beginning that she should never step foot inside the prison walls or in any other facility that the prisoners would be using, but that didn't stop Catherine! When the first prison basketball game was held she insisted on going. She walked into the auditorium with her three beautiful children and sat in the stands with the hardcore criminals. Other guests came up to her afterwards and asked, "How dare you sit with these men? Why do you take your little children in there?" And her reply was, "My husband and I are going to take care of these men, and I believe they will take care of me! I don't have to worry!"

She even insisted on getting acquainted with the records of the men. She discovered that one of the men convicted of murder was blind, so she paid him a visit. She stepped into the cold cell and sat down next to this man. Holding his hand in hers she warmly said, "Do

you read braille?" "What's braille?" he asked. "Don't you know? It is a way that you can read with your fingers," she explained. "Well, I've never heard of it," he replied. "I'll teach you then!" she enthused. And she taught that blind killer how to read braille. Years later he would weep in love for her.

Later Catherine found that there was a deaf mute in the prison, so she went to the school to learn sign language. Soon she was communicating with him through the use of her hands. Many said that Catherine Lawes was the body of Jesus Christ that came alive again at Sing Sing Prison from 1921 to 1937.

Then one evening the car in which she was riding went out of control and she was killed. The next morning her husband did not come to work, so the acting warden came in his place. In an instant the whole prison knew something was wrong. When they heard the news that their beloved lady had died, everyone wept.

The following day her body was resting in a casket in her home, three quarters of a mile from the prison. As the acting warden took his early morning walk, he was shocked to see a large crowd of the toughest, hardest-looking criminals gathering like a herd of animals at the main gate. It looked as if they were ready to launch a riot. He walked over to the group and instead of seeing hostility in their eyes he saw tears of grief and sadness. He knew how much they loved and admired Catherine. He turned and faced the men. "Alright men, you can go. Just be sure and check in!" Then he opened the gate without another word and a parade of more than 100 criminals walked, without a guard, three quarters of a mile to stand in line to pay their respects to Catherine Lawes. And every one of them checked in that night. *Every one! It's amazing what one life can do when it has the Spirit of Christ within.* Catherine Lawes believed there were no hopeless cases, only hopeless thinkers!

The warden's wife had the courage to take her little children and sit among murderers and rapists; a blond boy ripped off the house of a preacher two years ago, but had the courage to admit what he did and ask for forgiveness. Do you have courage? How much nerve do you have? Do you have enough courage to trust God as He comes to you and says: "I believe in you! I have a dream for your life!" Do you have the courage to step into tomorrow? Do you dare to step into the future? God is there waiting with Jesus Christ and He wants to tell you what a beautiful person you can become.

Let me tell you something. I made a discovery 22

years ago while ringing doorbells in this community. My wife was the only member and we wanted to start a church. We picked a slogan: A church that can put strong wings on weary hearts.

I would ring a doorbell and ask, "Are you an active member of a local church?" They would say, "Yes, we go to the Methodist Church." Then I would say, "Good, God bless you. Keep on going, they need every member they can get." Then I'd go to the next house and ask the same question. And they would say, "Yes, we go to the local Roman Catholic Church." "Good," I would say. "They need every member they can get." Or they would say, "We go to the Jewish Synagogue."

Then I would come to a house and ask once again, "Are you an active member of a local church?" And they would say, "No we don't belong to a church." And then I would say, "Do you have a faith?" And they would say, "No." And that's when I got to talk to them about Jesus Christ! They would usually invite me in and I would quickly look around. The house was generally neat, the lawn was kept up and the furnishings were nice. And as I looked into their eyes I saw beautiful people! I would look into the faces of these beautiful people and ask, "Why does a beautiful person like you not go to church?" They would usually come up with some excuse or say that they just never discovered it. That's when I had a revelation.

God said to me: "Robert Schuller, you are a Christian. The person you just talked to is not a Christian. Let me tell you that being a Christian does not mean that you are a better person than a non-Christian." That was kind of shocking! The second revelation was: "Bob, many non-Christian people are more beautiful than some Christian church members." And I accepted that. And then God said: "But, Schuller, you are a more beautiful person today because you are a Christian than if you were not a Christian! And these people, who are beautiful people even though they are non-Christians, will become even more beautiful if they will accept Jesus Christ into their lives."

Any person will become a more beautiful person if he accepts Jesus Christ into his life. I invite you to dare to step forward and accept Jesus Christ. We are still in the early flush of a new year. Decide now to walk with Christ!

# 3

## The Courage To Face Your Future

I want to ask you three questions. They were inspired by God when I was called upon to deliver a message at Hubert Humphrey's funeral. The questions have a universal application. First of all, what is courage? Second, why do we exalt courage? And third, where can you get it?

### I. What Is Courage?

We can all understand what courage is when we see a soldier fighting for our freedom as he heads for the front line. We can understand courage when we see a fire truck speeding down the street and the fireman climbing his ladder. We can understand courage when we see the police officer rushing through the black of night to protect someone from being assaulted by a mad man. That is a form of courage that we can all understand.

The Bible exalts that kind of courage! The words, "fear not" appear in the Bible 365 times. Once for every day of the year!

But there are different types and levels of courage. There is, of course, the courage to love. It takes a great deal of courage to love because when you really love someone you become emotionally involved and that means you've made a choice! You have made an emotional commitment. Now you are committed to something and you run the risk of being rejected. People often ask me, "Dr. Schuller, why isn't there more love in the world?" And my immediate reply is, "You are asking the wrong question. The right question to ask is, 'Why don't more people dare to love?' " It takes courage to love because when you love you get involved! And when you do that, you are liable to be swept away, and before you realize it, you've made a deep commitment!

There are many people, today, who are afraid of marriage. People are living together instead of going through the marriage ceremony. They offer several reasons for their behavior, but at a deeper level, they are afraid of marriage because they are afraid to make a commitment to continuity. *It takes courage to love!* Ultimately, love is going to have to lead to a commitment. Love is shallow until you are willing to make a commitment to continuity—to love even when the skin is wrinkled and the hair is white! It takes courage to love!

Another form of courage is the courage to forgive! You will not love long if you cannot forgive quickly. In all of our interpersonal relationships, we will not love long unless we have the capacity to forgive quickly. That includes my love for God. Forgive God? Yes. There are people today who are atheists because at the deepest level they are really angry at God. Maybe as children they cried out and didn't get what they thought God should have given them, so they became angry towards Him. Or perhaps they experienced a crisis in a personal relationship and they cried out to God, asking for something but God appeared to be silent. They've never really brought themselves to a point where they are willing to forgive God and start over again.

When you forgive, you are not saying that the other party has done anything wrong. That's why you can forgive God. Because forgiveness means you are able to accept what comes your way. It's easy to forgive somebody if they are guilty and they repent, but it's not easy to accept some things that life puts before you. That kind of forgiveness takes courage. To love requires courage! It takes courage to forgive and unless you are able to forgive quickly, your love will never last long in any relationship.

Some of you may harbor a resentment against a husband, wife, child, teacher, or maybe an employer. You just don't dare to forgive. Part of it is the fact that if you really forgave that person, you'd have to swallow your pride. Only brave people dare to be humble! It takes courage to love. It takes courage to forgive because, you see, you run the risk of rejection, ridicule and scorn from those whose scales of justice are too heavy and scales of mercy are too light.

What is courage? Well, we can now understand the courage of the fireman and policeman; the courage of the husband and wife who go to the altar to make a permanent commitment; and the courage of forgiveness. But there is another level of courage that I could not understand for a long time. This was the courage of a person who bravely fights a terminal illness. My secretary died of cancer after battling it for twelve years. I remember people saying to me, "Bob, Lois is so brave," and I have never really understood that statement.

I first met Hubert Humphrey about five years ago. I received a letter from him saying that he and his wife, Muriel, watched the Hour of Power and that it was a great help to them on a very deep and personal level. He told me to stop in and see him the next time I was in Washington so I did! When I found his office I told his secretary who I was and she smiled and said, "Oh, Dr. Schuller, he really wants to see you!" Then she had a member of his staff take me to the Senate Chamber where Senator Humphrey was speaking.

He was finishing just as I entered the room. When he rushed over and warmly embraced me, I didn't know exactly what to say, so I handed him one of the little gold cards with the possibility thinkers' creed printed on it. "What's this?" Hubert asked. And I told him to read it. In his strong and sturdy voice he began:

When faced with a mountain I will not quit, I will keep on striving until I climb over, find a pass through, tunnel underneath or simply stay and turn the mountain into a gold mine, with God's help.

Tears filled his eyes before he could finish. This was only the beginning of what would become a deep, personal relationship.

People have said it through the years and I affirm it today—Hubert had great courage! People who fight a terminal illness, and keep on fighting bravely, have courage! I have always admired their perseverance. I have always admired their faith. But I used to say, "Why do you call it courage? What's so brave about it? Perseverance? Yes. Tough? Of course. But courageous? But why do you say it's courage when somebody's fighting a battle of cancer?"

It's courageous because a person who fights a brave battle with a terminal illness is making a commitment! There can be no courage unless there is a choice between alternatives. And the person who is fighting a terminal illness is making a choice between two alternatives. One is to overdose and slip away quickly. The other is to hang in there as bravely and optimistically as possible until God stops the heartbeat. When you're faced with alternatives, choose the one where the personal price is high, but where the reward in terms of inspiration to those around you is also high. That's courage!

## II. Why Do We Exalt Courage?

Because every person who chooses to be brave inspires the rest of the human race! That's why! The entire human family is exalted, honored, and dignified as a species when some other fellow creature fights their brave battle and we can say, "That's my relative or that's my friend!"

In my recent book, *Peace of Mind Through Possibility Thinking,* I tell about a conversation I had with a good friend, Abby. She writes her own column in the newspaper, called "Dear Abby." We were at dinner together in Beverly Hills and I was telling her about our ministry and the suicides that we prevent through our 24-hour, life-line, Christian, telephone counseling program. She was surprised when I told her that we operate the longest standing, continually operating, New Hope Telephone Counseling Center right here on the campus of the Garden Grove Community Church. I told her how proud we were of the fact that no ministry saves more lives than we do!

Abby's reply was a question, "Dr. Schuller, what's so wrong about suicide?" "What's wrong with suicide," I replied, "is that it's the easy way out. Your friends and relatives are the ones left behind to live with the terrible hurt. They carry the scars for the rest of their lives!"

Your life and mine will be judged before Almighty God on this question: "When I was faced with alternatives did I choose the brave way?" And if I did, I uplifted the collective level of social self-esteem in the process. That's why we exalt courage!

I have never met Charlotte Valente but I sure want to some day. I became acquainted with her story through some literature that I received from the Children's Hospital in Los Angeles.

Mary Ames Anderson, now the retired editor, said if she were to pick one child in the Children's Hospital that inspired her more than anybody else, it would have to be Charlotte Valente. And here's Mary Anderson's beautiful story.

"I was walking through the corridor of the children's hospital in 1953 when I heard a young voice say, 'Here I am!' I stopped and turned to see where the voice was coming from. And that's when I saw a little, girl, barely two years old, lying in bed hugging her teddy bear. She seemed so young to be speaking so clearly. Both of her tiny legs were hanging in the air, in traction. 'Well, hello!' I enthused. Smiling, she asked, 'How are you today?' But before I could answer she interrupted, 'I have brittle bones. This one is broken. Last time it was

that one,' she said as she pointed to her right leg. 'But this time it is this one. I have had 22 fractures!'

"By the age of six Charlotte had been in and out of the hospital 85 times. She has a rare disease which causes her bones to break very easily. She had over 200 fractures by the time she was ten but she is a delightful little girl, always smiling and very positive.

"I only saw her cry three times," Mrs. Anderson wrote. "Once when she fractured her arm the day before her sister's wedding and she had to stay in the hospital. The other time was when she made a community appeal to urge people to give so crippled children could walk. 'I will never walk,' Charlotte said in her plea, 'but hundreds of others can walk if only you'll help!' Charlotte couldn't walk because by the time she reached puberty the disease arrested itself and her normal development had been permanently distorted. She would probably never weigh more than fifty pounds in her entire lifetime. But this brave young girl didn't cry until she was recognized by community leaders. And do you know why? Because they gave her a typewriter—the one material thing that she'd wanted ever since she was a child. She didn't want a bike because she could never ride one. She wanted a typewriter! And when she was presented this gift she cried and cried. 'I'm the luckiest girl in the whole world!' she exclaimed." *That's courage!*

Charlotte went on to high school and graduated. Then she picked a university that had ramps equipped for the handicapped. She was accepted and graduated four years later Cum Laude! But Charlotte did not stop there! She went on to law school and passed the state bar exam. All 50 pounds of her!

Courage! What is it? It's the back side of love. That's what it is. It's the other side of the coin. Somebody who loves life enough to want to live every minute no matter how costly it may be! Somebody so much in love with life that he will fight everyday through the pain of chemotherapy and radiation. Somebody who loves persons enough to be willing to say, "I take you for better, for worse, for richer or poorer, in sickness and in health, till death do us part." Somebody who loves God enough to believe that He will never abandon you!

### III. Where Do You Get This Kind of Courage?

You get it from the Ideal One more than anywhere else. At a very deep level this is what you and I need. I have it and I hope I can share it with you. We all need an Ideal One! One ideal person who lives in our minds and loves us. One to whom we can relate. One who lifts us and inspires us. And for me, that Ideal One is Jesus Christ!

What happens to a human being who carries within

his mind some person who is Perfect and Ideal? The love of life comes in and that brings courage! The late Ozzie Nelson used to tell this story about his son, Ricky.

He said, "Ricky was just a young boy when he begged me to let his friend Walter come over and spend the weekend with him. After much persistence I gave in. On the day that Walter was to come over I got off work a little early so I could play with the boys. We went into the backyard and started throwing a football around. I was getting really good when Ricky said, 'Hey, dad, you're great!' And Walter piped in and exclaimed, 'Gee, Mr. Nelson, you've got a pretty good arm, but not as good as my dad.' When it came to dinnertime I carved the roast so beautifully with thin and even slices. 'Look at those nice slices, Walter,' I bragged. 'You carve the roast pretty good, Mr. Nelson,' Walter enthused, 'but you should see my dad do it!' I couldn't believe it! I couldn't do anything as well as this kid's father.

"Well, when their bedtime came I decided to tell one of my best stories. Their eyes were popping out of their heads! 'That's a great story, Mr. Nelson, but my dad is one of the best storytellers there is!' And the next day the same thing happened, no matter what we did together. I was starting to dislike a man I'd never even met. I couldn't wait for Walter's mother to pick him up so I could find out about this super-dad! When she came to the door I said, 'Hi! I'm delighted to meet you.' 'How was Walter?' she asked. 'Oh, just great,' I exclaimed. 'I'd sure like to meet your husband. He must be something else!' 'Oh, no,' she said, 'has Walter been talking about his dad again? You see, Walter was only three years old when his dad was killed at Corregidor.'" That little boy had an Ideal One that lived within him. His image of his father gave him courage.

My Ideal One died before I was born—at Calvary! But He lives today! His name is Jesus! That's where I get my nerve. He lives in me and He wants to live in you!

# Discover
# The Miracles
# In Your Life

# 1

## What Is a Miracle?

I believe a hundred million miracles are happening every day, but only those who look for them will spot them on life's way. A miracle is a beautiful thing that happens in our life because God loves us, cares for us and did something beautiful for us.

The Psalmist wrote,

"Surely goodness and mercy shall follow me all the days of my life." (Psalm 23:6)

God has miracles planned for you every day. The truth is, God bestows His miracles even upon people who don't believe in Him. (The only thing is, they don't call them miracles!)

As I was traveling recently, I took notes on the comments that people made. I heard people say: "An odd coincidence" was the phrase one person used. Somebody else said, "I had a marvelous serendipity." I also heard, "A wonderful thing happened yesterday." "You'll never guess who I ran into today," and "You'll never believe what I experienced."

The world calls these things coincidences, serendipities and unexpected things. I call them miracles—acts of God. A hundred million miracles are happening every day, but only those who have faith can spot them on life's way.

My definition of a miracle is some wonderful thing that happens to us that we can't explain, where all the odds say it shouldn't work out that way, but it still worked out beautifully. By all odds it should have ended up catastrophically or disastrously, but by some stroke of divine providence over which we had no control, it worked out so much better.

God is good to all of us. There are a hundred million miracles happening every day. If you can't count miracles in your life every day, it doesn't mean God isn't doing something good for you. It does mean that you are not spiritually capable at that point in time of sensing the goodness that is there.

I want to try and develop within you the skill of getting into the habit of counting your miracles every day. In order to do that we must understand what a miracle is and how you can spot them. Let me teach you now how to spot a miracle.

As some of you know, I maintain a private little place down the coast here in Southern California where I've moved my library and where, alone in my times of prayer, meditation, study, solitude and writing, I can commune with God and, hopefully, come through with material that may be God's message for you.

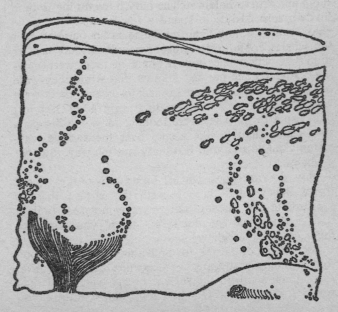

Now I happen to have a love affair with the great California grey whale. They are massive, beautiful, marvelous beasts of the deep. Every winter, starting in December and through January, these massive beasts come from their home in the Alaskan waters and migrate down right along the coast. From their home in Alaska they go all the way down to Mexico until they reach a point where the temperature of the water approximates the temperature of the womb of the female cow. At that point she gives birth to her calf. And since the temperature of the water is close to the temperature of the womb, the calf is able to survive the birth, and then move out of the Mexican waters heading back up the coast until they arrive once more at their home in the cold waters off the coast of Alaska. By the time they've reached that point, the calf's body has adjusted to the change of the temperature of the water.

So it happens year after year; the cycle goes on and on. And I have become, I must say with all modesty, quite an expert whale watcher. I have from time to time invited close friends to spend a few hours in my little study. And I say, "When you're there, be sure to spot the whales." And often, they come back and say, "I didn't see any whales today. None of them were moving." And I smile because I know that while they were looking out over that vast expanse of ocean, there were whales moving right underneath the surface. They just didn't spot them! They were looking for some big massive beasts, floating like a ship over the surface, geysering like Old Faithful. But that's not the way you spot a whale.

How do you spot a whale? First; *believe* they're out there! Believe that there beneath the surface there is life lurking and moving that you may not see. Believe that! Even when you don't spot them, you don't see them, continue to believe!

Secondly, don't look for something dramatic. Look for something that appears to be quite natural, like an exceptional swirl on the surface of the water and then watch for a puff of fog. It'll look like a little cloud,

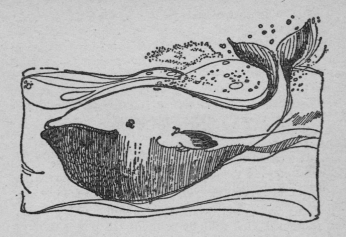

blown by the wind. Keep watching now, keep looking, and eventually you'll see a hump of black and maybe even a whole tail, eight feet wide from tip to tip, glistening white, waving in the sun, before it plummets down and disappears.

You look for miracles the way you look for whales. Don't expect something big, dramatic and unnatural. Expect something quite ordinary, yet surrounded by mysterious circumstances that are wonderful. Then, eventually, you will see with the passing of days, or weeks, or months, or even years, that that seemingly trivial event, encounter, circumstance or experience turned out to be a pivotal point in your whole life! Your whole destiny, it appears now, hinged upon that event over which you had no control whatever! And looking back, you can only say, "It was an act of God. It was a miracle!"

# 2

## *The Miracle Maker*

Now that we have defined miracles, let's move on to an understanding of what God is like. God is not a big boss who throws His power around. To understand God's miracles you have to understand that He has limited His own power. Mark this carefully: God's power is restrained. God willfully restrains His power in three ways: First, by the nature of nature; second, by the nature of man; and third, by the nature of Himself.

When God built this world, He built into this universe certain natural laws, like the laws of gravity. With these laws, God has limited His power. This in no way diminishes God's power or character, because it is voluntary on His part. So God's power is limited. This is no indignity to His character: God's decision to restrain His power only glorifies Him more. For remember this if you forget everything else:

## POWER RESTRAINED IS
## POWER IMPROVED!

It is because God is holy that He restrains His power. Power restrained is power improved! Unrestrained power means there are no ethics. You bulldoze, you push to get your way. Power restrained is power improved. No person will ever be able to jump off a building and on the way down say, "God, I'm going to test your power. Please let me fall and not get hurt." It doesn't work that way, for God restrains His power by the nature of nature.

He also restrains His power by the nature of man. He made you and He made me with a certain degree of free will. He wants persons; not puppets. He could have created you and me and every other human being so that we would be nothing more than brilliant computers responding to a God who sits in heaven at the master control pushing these buttons, and everything goes along beautifully. There would be no sin. There would be no injustice. There would be no Nazi holocaust. There would be none of this. The only thing is, there would be no persons, only computers, if there was no free will.

The nature of man and the nature of nature restrains God's power. That's why if you could cut off your arm, and then look for a miracle to grow out a new arm, it'll never happen.

The nature of man, the nature of nature, and finally

God limits His power by His own nature. God respects the dignity of persons in such a way that He will not overpower your will against your own decision to act.

Let me illustrate. If you decide that you want something and you do not care about the Ten Commandments or the word of God or the teachings of Jesus— God will let you have your way. He respects your independence. That's His nature. He will advise you, He will direct you, He will lead you, He will enlighten you, but it is ultimately your decision! If you choose not to trust God—of course His Miracle Power is reduced.

So, as we look at miracles, keep this in mind: What is a miracle? A miracle is a beautiful act of God's providence moving into life, and there are many of them happening every day.

When my only son was a little boy, he learned to

drive the car in the empty drive-in church parking area through the week. He would sit in my lap, put his tiny little hands on the wheel, and drive. Unknown to him, I would hold the bottom of the steering wheel. He would manipulate the curves so well and put the car right into the correct parking space, and he would say, "Didn't I do a good job, Daddy? All by myself." And I would say, "Yes, son, you sure did." But my hand was always at the bottom of the wheel.

I call that a miracle. And only God knows how many times you were spared from a crisis because He kept His hand, unseen, at the bottom of the wheel.

Count your miracles every day. Become an expert miracle spotter, and you'll have something to laugh about every day of your life.

# 3

## *Count Your Miracles Every Day*

There is not a doubt in my mind that a hundred million miracles are happening every day. But only those who have faith will spot them on life's way.

The problem is not that miracles aren't happening today. The problem is, we just don't see them, spot them and recognize them when they occur.

Of course, there are miracles that are easy to spot. Anne Fischer once shared with me how she survived the Jewish extermination of the Second World War. She was the only survivor of eight children.

While she was in one Nazi camp, the man she was engaged to before the whole outbreak occurred, an architectural student named Benno Fischer, was the only one of his family of ten children to survive the Nazi extermination of Jews in another camp. Both—unknown to the other—survived the holocaust. Years later they met each other. A miracle!

Let me tell you how that meeting occurred. It happened in Stuttgart, Germany. I said to Benno, "Benno, you are Polish. What in the world made you go to Stuttgart? Did you suspect Anne was alive?"

"I never thought she was alive," he answered. "I went to Munich to look up an old friend and I found him. He was alive and he said to me, 'Benno, I'm going to Stuttgart.' And I asked him, 'What are you going to

do in Stuttgart?' He replied, 'My mother survived and I want to see her.' I said, 'I have news for you. Your father died in my arms in the concentration camp. Let me go with you and I will tell your mother how her husband died.' "

So Benno went with this friend to Stuttgart, Germany, called on the mother and shared with her the story of her husband's passing at camp. She thanked him for the love and the tenderness he gave to her husband in his last days and hours of life. And then, his mission accomplished, he went to catch a bus to go back to Poland, never again expecting to come to Germany. At the bus stop, he saw a girl who looked familiar. He paced back and forth. He could not believe what he saw. She looked just like the girl he was engaged to marry four years before. And then she, suspecting she was being eyed by a stranger, turned around, and they fell into each other's arms! As Benno himself said, "It was a miracle of God. I had never been to Stuttgart before or since."

What brought him there? It was a miracle! Many of us have had meetings over which we have had no control. We didn't plan it. We didn't stage it. We didn't manipulate it. It just happened!

There isn't a week that I don't get letters from people

all over the United States saying to me, "Dr. Schuller, I just happened to turn on the television because I wanted to look at a football game or maybe a movie that was coming on. I was turning the dial and suddenly stopped for a moment on your program. And I started listening. And the odd thing is, I've never been very religious. I don't go to church. I don't claim to be a believer. The miracle is, I listened to what was being said. Dr. Schuller, I tuned in the following week and then the next week. Today, I know God. I met Him; He's real."

The world calls it chance. Positive thinking people call it, not chance, *but God!* Which leads me back to the promise in Psalm 23:

"Surely goodness and mercy shall follow me all the days of my life" (Ps. 23:6).

Think about that, *all the days of your life.* Another way of saying that is every single day of my life God's goodness and mercy is going to be shown to me. That means that there is not a single day in your human, earthly existence where God does not do *something* beautiful for you. Now you may not see it, you may not know it, you may not even recognize that this is an act of God within you, but that does not invalidate His activity.

I watched a television program the other morning, and they were discussing the photography of Weston, now deceased, who was obviously one of the greatest photographers of our time. As a backdrop for the conversation, they had an enlargement of one of his famous photographs. It showed a beautiful sculptured mountain and in the foreground were three unadorned telephone poles. A novice would look at it and say it's a picture of three telephone poles, in front of a hill. The truth is it was a most unique, creative, dramatic, beautiful composition. As the panel was discussing the picture the television interviewer said, "Couldn't anybody take a camera, go out there and snap that same picture? What's so great about Weston? Couldn't anybody take that same

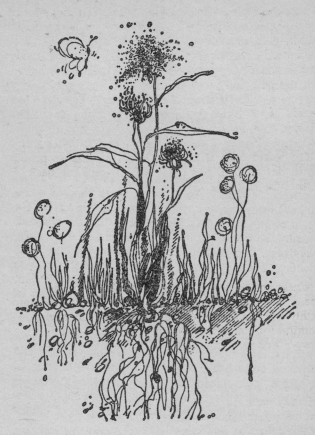

picture?" One of the critics said, "No! No! Nobody else could do it." "Why not?" asked the interviewer. And the critic replied, "Nobody else would see it." And I think he's right.

And I thought of that recently as I was driving down a canyon road. There in a ditch, stood a young man with a camera, photographing what looked like just another dirty, old scroungy, seedy weed. But he *saw* something! That's the kind of vision you need to be a miracle spotter. Start counting your miracles every day!

# 4

## Time To Spot
## Your Miracles

Why don't we see all these miracles that are happening all around us? I think I can answer it this way: Have you ever been hospitalized, maybe for a few days, or a week or more? An amazing thing happens when you have recovered enough and the hour has arrived for you to return home. As you come out of the hospital, suddenly the whole world looks different—cars, people, sky, trees. You notice flowers blooming that were blooming when you went into the hospital, but you failed to notice them before. Everything looks different. You have a tremendous, almost ethereal dimension of awareness.

Let's take another illustration: You've left on a vacation. You've probably lived in your apartment or your house for some time. But you've been on vacation and when you come back, it suddenly looks so different— the rooms, the furniture, the house, everything. You see things you didn't see before. There is, for want of a better word, a heightened sensitivity in the area of human perception.

How do you explain it? It's really quite simple. A blanket of daily, accumulated anxieties, fears, depressions, jealousies, problems and difficulties were temporarily lifted. What blinds us to the trees, the flowers, the clouds, the sky, the sparkle in the eye of someone we're talking to? What blinds us to the miracles that God is performing? It is our negative emotional attitude, our fears and our worries, our concerns and our anxieties. It's the bad news we've just heard or the bad news we

are expecting when we go to the mailbox or when the telephone rings or when there's a knock at the door.

So you see, it's not God's problem, it's yours and mine. It's not that God isn't doing anything, it's that we have allowed ourselves to react negatively to life's daily problems to the point where we no longer see the flowers blooming or spot the miracles that are happening all around us. It's not, you see, a matter of having problems or not having problems, it's a matter of how we react to them.

A hundred million miracles are happening every day. It happens in those chance meetings, those unplanned encounters.

My friend Paul Harvey, whom many of you know from radio and television newscasting, told a story recently about a young man who was only four years old, and I relate to this story. I'll tell you in a minute why and how I relate to it on a very personal level.

There was a mother whose name was Mrs. Sutton. She lived in Hawaii and she came to visit America with her two sons. The year was 1919. She was traveling on

a train with her sons across the United States when her oldest boy had an epileptic seizure. She had to take care of him, but she didn't know what to do with her four-year-old son Richard. There was a stranger sitting across the aisle and she asked, "Sir, excuse me, could you watch my son?" And the man said, "Sure."

So the little boy sat with him. They talked while the mother took care of her older son. When the seizures were gone and everything was calmed down, she came back. The distinguished gentleman, who had proved to be a very good baby-sitter, said, "You've got a nice little boy there. You know, when he grows up, he ought to be a lawyer. He's a good talker. A smart little fellow, too. In fact, he ought to go to Stanford University. That's the best place to go. When he grows up, you just let me know and I'll see if I can't help him get into Stanford."

The years passed. It was now 1931. The young boy never forgot what he heard that man on the train say to him, "You ought to be a lawyer when you grow up. And you ought to go to Stanford." When he graduated from high school, he wrote the man, because this man was now very famous. The boy wrote to him and said, "You may not remember me, but you said when I got ready to go to college, you thought I ought to go to Stanford and I ought to be a lawyer and you'd help." Well, Herbert Hoover got Richard Sutton admitted to Stanford, and also lined up a summer job so the boy could earn money to pay for his tuition. The boy was a successful student.

When he graduated, he wrote to Herbert Hoover again and said, "Now, sir, what can I do for you?" Hoover, as you know, was a Republican. He said, "Go

back to Hawaii, enter politics, and I ask you to do only one thing. Run as a Republican for office, and keep running until you win. If you forget everything else I tell you in life, *keep running until you win.*" Well, giving that young graduate advice to go to Hawaii and enter politics as a Republican was not exactly a formula for success. As many of you know, that state has been very heavily Democratic. But this young boy was so devoted, he ran for office as a Republican and lost. He ran again and lost. Three times, four times, five times he ran for the legislature. And lost every time. Everybody said he should quit. But he said, "No, I owe it to that man, Herbert Hoover. He told me to keep running until I win." So he kept running. Seven times, eight times, nine times, ten times, eleven times, and he lost every time. Then came November, 1974, and he decided he was going to run again. Well, you know what happened in November, 1974? In Hawaii, like in most states, it was a Democratic sweep, and this fellow was still running as a Republican. But miracles do happen— he won! One of the few Republicans to win, but he

won. He is today in the legislature of Hawaii. Ike Sutton is his name. He's 56 years old, I believe. He had eleven defeats, but he would not quit!

Keep running until you win. He was four years old at that chance meeting that set the direction of his whole life.

I was four years old when my uncle came home from China and met me at the gate of our Iowa farm home. I was born while he was over there, and he said, "So you're Robert, are you? You ought to be a preacher when you grow up." And then he ran into the house to embrace his sister, forgetting all about me, not giving another thought to the words he left with me. But I was impressed in that moment. That's when God gave me my calling. And that was over 40 years ago.

Chance meeting, chance greeting, off-the-cuff remarks. This week, today, this very moment, God is trying to say something to you and that's a miracle. What is a miracle? It's when God decides to personally move into your life and do something with you. What God is saying to you now is this:

## IT TAKES TWO TO MAKE A MIRACLE.

God can't do it alone. You have to cooperate. You have to respond, positively, in faith. *It takes two to make a miracle!*

Probably the greatest miracle that ever happened in your life is happening right now. You are becoming a believer. You are asking Jesus Christ to come into your life. You are ready to make a lasting, life-changing decision to become a more beautiful person.

How do you spot a miracle? If you want to spot a miracle, just look for a mountain in your life. Look for a problem or a difficulty, because often the first way God reaches us is in a moment of pain. There is not gain without pain! Every problem is loaded with opportunities.

If you have a problem, I predict, it's the beginning of

a miracle. Why does God allow us to run into mountains? Some mountains are there to block us so that we won't run madly ahead and get ourselves into trouble. If a mountain is there to keep us from going into enemy territory, then the mountain indeed has been turned into a miracle.

Together with God, you can turn any problem, any mountain into a miracle. The way to spot the miracle is to stop dwelling on the problem, and start looking for the miracles. Use your eyes of faith.

Possibly the greatest miracle that ever happened in

your life is happening right now. You are becoming a believer. You are asking Jesus Christ to come into your life and give you eyes of faith. You are ready to make a lasting, life-changing decision to become a more beautiful person—to become a child of God.

Years from now you will look back on that moment of decision and you'll say, "Wow! I don't know why I read that book. I don't even know why I bought it. Isn't it odd?" And I'll say to you, "No, it isn't odd. It's God!"

Be a miracle spotter!